Dispute Board Manual

A Guide to Best Practices and Procedures

The Dispute Resolution Board Foundation

DRBF

Fostering Common Sense Dispute Resolution Worldwide

Dispute Board Manual: A Guide to Best Practices and Procedures
Dispute Resolution Board Foundation

Designed, produced, and published by SPARK Publications
SPARKpublications.com
Charlotte, North Carolina, USA

Softcover, November 2019, ISBN: 978-1-943070-68-8
E-book, November 2019, ISBN: 978-1-943070-69-5
Library of Congress Control Number: 2019913499

Table of Contents

Section 1
Background on Dispute Boards

Chapter

Section 2
Dispute Board Concepts

Chapter

Section 3
Establishing Dispute Boards

Chapter

Section 4
Dispute Boards – Implementation and Process

Chapter

Acknowledgments

This guide to practices and procedures in dispute prevention and resolution has been compiled and reviewed by a dedicated group of Dispute Resolution Board Foundation (DRBF) leaders and supporters.

They have given their time, enthusiasm and specialist knowledge to make this manual a comprehensive guide to current best practices, lessons learned and trends in the use of Dispute Boards worldwide. The DRBF is grateful for their contributions as well as the guidance and input of DRBF leadership.

Lead Editors
Graham Easton
Ann Russo

Lead Reviewers/Contributors
Kurt Dettman
Steven Goldstein
Lindy Patterson
James Perry

Contributors: Romano Allione, Adrian Bastianelli, Warren Bullock, William Edgerton, Ronald Finlay, Ferdinand Fourie, Jeremy Glover, Nicholas Gould, Andrew Griffiths, Leo Grutters, Wilburt Hinton II, Douglas Holen, Gordon Jaynes, Harold McKittrick, Christopher Miers, Thomas Peterson, James Phillips, Marcela Radovic, Robert Rubin, Geoff Smith, Robert Smith and Barry Tozer.

Editorial Assistance
Nichole Thompson
Susan Shackelford
SPARK Publications

Special thanks to California Department of Transportation, Colorado Department of Transportation and Washington State Department of Transportation for providing details on their fee structures and rates for Dispute Board members.

The DRBF also acknowledges in appreciation the authors of the original "Dispute Review Board Manual," A.A. Mathews, R.M. Matyas, R.J. Smith and P.E. Sperry, published in 1996; and the authors of the DRBF Manual, "Practices and Procedures," W.B. Baker, P.M. Douglass, W.W. Edgerton, and P.E. Sperry, published in 2007. These two publications are the foundation on which this 2019 Manual has been constructed.

Preface

The Dispute Resolution Board Foundation (DRBF) created this manual to provide an authoritative explanation of the Dispute Board (DB) process, and to serve as a reference guide for users of the process throughout the world.

The guide addresses the fundamentals of successful DBs and their important role in both avoiding and resolving disputes among the contracting parties on large and complex projects.

As the DB process has developed since the mid-1970s, different terms have arisen to suit particular variations. These variations share the same structure and fundamental purpose: *to encourage dispute avoidance and to assist in timely and cost-effective resolution of disputes for the duration of a project.*

This manual uses the term "Dispute Board," or its abbreviation, "DB," to refer to variations of the process, except when citing other names for context and educational purposes.

In the United States and Canada, the most common terms are "Dispute Review Board" or "Dispute Resolution Board." In Australia, there is a preference for the term "Dispute Avoidance Board." For projects using FIDIC forms of contract or institutional rules, the most common terms are "Dispute Adjudication Board" or "Dispute Avoidance and Adjudication Board." This manual addresses any notable differences in procedures under these variations.

Given the widespread use of the DB process, additional terminology issues occur based on local language, industry terminology, contracting procedures and cultural differences. You may refer to this manual's Glossary for details.

This guide updates the DRBF's previous manual and explains practices and procedures that have evolved in the application of DBs. Special attention is given to recommended best practices, as well as cautions about modifications to the process which may be acceptable only in certain circumstances, or which are not recommended.

Early publications providing guidance on DBs were published in 1989 and 1991 by the American Society of Civil Engineers. In 1996, McGraw-Hill published the "Construction Dispute Review Board Manual," written by the founders of the DRBF. The DRBF published its first "Practice and Procedures Manual" in 2004 and updated it in 2007.

Available Resources

The DRBF maintains copies of best-practice forms of contract and other forms used in Dispute Board practice on the DRBF website, www.drb.org. There is also a library of articles and conference papers, a member resume directory, and other resources. For additional information, contact the DRBF by email at info@drb.org or by phone at +1 980-265-2367.

1

Background on Dispute Boards

Chapter 1
A Brief History of Dispute Boards

Dispute Boards were conceived within the construction industry. Traditionally, the construction industry has resolved contractual disputes on projects using methods that range from litigation to alternative resolution processes such as arbitration, mediation and adjudication. The most recent and successful development is the introduction of Dispute Boards (DBs) into the contract and dispute management process.

In the 1950s, competition for public construction contracts in the United States became intense, and contractors were forced to accept lower profit margins. Moreover, construction projects became larger and more complex with many parties performing different aspects of the work.

The construction process also was burdened with nontechnical demands such as environmental regulations, governmental and socio-economic requirements, and public interest group pressures. Furthermore, internal procedures and statutory or regulatory impediments limited the capacity of public owners and employers to settle disputes.

The net result of these factors, coupled with the financial instability of many contractors with tight margins, required contracting parties to pursue all available means to protect their commercial position. A growing body of lawyers and consultants stood ready to assist them.

As the trend to resolve disputes by formal litigation increased and relationships became more adversarial, the construction industry sought more cost-effective and practical solutions.

Arbitration became popular because it was less expensive and faster than litigation. However, as a dispute resolution process, it too became costly, time consuming and adversarial. Although commercial arbitration continues to offer certain benefits unavailable in litigation — primarily the use of neutral parties experienced in the field from which the dispute arises — the cost and time demands of arbitration today can often exceed that of complex litigation. The ensuing movement away from litigation and arbitration led to alternative dispute resolution (ADR) processes such as mediation, and subsequently to development of the DB concept.

Birth of the Dispute Board

In 1972, the U.S. National Committee on Tunneling Technology sponsored a study of contracting practices throughout the world, to develop recommendations for improved contracting methods in the United States. The study concluded that the deleterious effect of disputes and litigation upon the efficiency of the construction process was a major cause of rapidly escalating construction costs. Results of the study were presented in the "Better Contracting for Underground Construction" report, published in 1974 — and the DB concept was born.

In 1975 within the U.S., the DB process was first used during construction of the second bore of the Eisenhower Tunnel for Interstate 70 in Colorado. The original DB members included Al Mathews, Palmer King and Charles McGraw.

Compared with previous dispute resolution processes, the DB process was an overwhelming success. The Board dealt with three significant disputes, yet the owner-contractor relationship remained cordial throughout construction, and all parties were satisfied with the final time and cost outcomes for the project. Other successful DBs soon followed, and the U.S. construction industry began to recognize the unique features of the DB process for managing and resolving disputes.

The American Society of Civil Engineers promoted the DB concept in the first edition of its manual, "Avoiding and Resolving Disputes During Construction," in 1989. This publication was updated and revised in 1991 by the Technical Committee on Contracting Practices of the Underground Technology Research Council. Notable among the 12 committee members were A.A. "Al" Mathews, P.E. "Joe" Sperry and Robert J. "Bob" Smith, three of the eventual founders of the Dispute Resolution Board Foundation (DRBF).

Dispute Boards go Global

As the success of the DB process became obvious, the use of DBs spread worldwide. The first DB outside the U.S. occurred in Honduras with the construction of the El Cajón Dam and Hydroelectric Plant in 1980. Other DBs soon followed internationally, encouraged by the support of governments, professional engineering associations and project-funding institutions such as the World Bank.

In the 1990s, several large international projects successfully utilized DBs, including the Channel Tunnel Project (U.K./France), the new Hong Kong International Airport and the Ertan Hydroelectric Project in China.

In January 1995, the World Bank published a new edition of its standard bidding document, "Procurement of Works," which provided the borrower with three options for the settlement of disputes, including the use of a three-person DB. The three-person DB was made mandatory for contracts in excess of US$50 million.

Later in 1995, the International Federation of Consulting Engineers (FIDIC) published the first edition of its "Orange Book," which introduced its Dispute Adjudication Board concept into FIDIC contracts.

In 1999, FIDIC introduced both standing and ad hoc DBs — the FIDIC "Red Book" providing for a standing DB and the Yellow and Silver books providing for an ad hoc DB (with the option for a standing DB). In 2017, all the FIDIC Rainbow Suite of Contracts underwent a significant review and now include the DB concept in its revised form of a Dispute Avoidance and Adjudication Board.

Meanwhile, the DB process took root in the 1990s with several state transportation agencies in the U.S., particularly in Florida and California. Encouraged by the performance and success of their DBs, these agencies began using DBs on all major construction projects.

International Growth

Since the mid-1990s, milestones in expansion of the DB process
have included adoption in 1997 by the Asian Development Bank
and the European Bank for Reconstruction & Development for their
internationally funded projects.

In 2004, the International Chamber of Commerce (ICC) introduced
its DB rules, which allowed users to choose between a Dispute Review
Board, a Dispute Adjudication Board and a Combined Dispute Board
(a hybrid allowing for nonbinding recommendations in some cases and
binding decisions in others). The ICC's rules were subsequently updated
in 2015 to incorporate, among other things, the concepts of dispute
avoidance and facilitation as part of the DB process.

In 2005, as part of the United Nations' Millennium Goals, the heads
of procurement of many development banks and multilateral lending
agencies ("MDBs") partnered with FIDIC to develop the "FIDIC MDB
Harmonised Conditions of Contract," or "Pink Book," which included a
DB process for both dispute avoidance and dispute resolution. Developing
countries now widely use these contract conditions, updated in 2010, for
major infrastructure projects. Subsequently, nine MDBs around the world
have adopted the DB process.

Also in 2005, the U.K.-based Institution of Civil Engineers published the
first edition of its "Dispute Resolution Board Procedures."

In Australia, the number of DBs has grown exponentially since 2005.
Most major public infrastructure projects now include a DB process
within their contractual framework, including several large Public Private
Partnership (PPP) contracts. Australia has also pioneered a trend away
from the traditional DB role of dispute resolution to a more proactive
form of DB, where the primary role is dispute avoidance.

Since 2008, Japan's International Cooperation Agency (JICA) has
actively promoted the use of DBs for overseas projects financed by JICA
Official Development Assistance loans, often called ODA loans. DBs are

a mandatory inclusion in JICA's procurement guidelines and standard bidding documents. JICA has also developed its own DB manual and conducted extensive training for DB members and users.

In South Africa, the Institution for Civil Engineering provided for both ad hoc and standing DBs in its 2010 edition of "General Conditions of Contract for Construction Works." These DBs reflect the current international trend in the DB process, emphasizing the proactive role of DBs in dispute avoidance as well as dispute resolution.

In 2014, the U.K. Chartered Institute of Arbitrators published the first edition of its international "Dispute Board Rules." These rules (as with the ICC's rules) extend the DB process beyond construction contracts to any medium- or long-term project, construction or otherwise.

Several other new forms of DB rules have recently appeared, some of which are yet to be widely used. For example, specific rules for the implementation of DBs have been published in South America, including in Peru, Brazil and Chile. In Indonesia, the government has recently introduced a new law allowing the use of DBs for dispute resolution on major public works projects.

DBs are increasingly being used within PPP projects, both at sponsor and project-delivery levels. There have also been hybrid DB rules developed for some large projects, often with multiple contracts. Examples are the London 2012 Olympics & Paralympics, the Rio 2016 Olympics & Paralympics, and the European Union's international nuclear fusion research and engineering megaproject called Joint Undertaking for ITER and the Development of Fusion Energy, best known as "Fusion for Energy (F4E)."

Today DBs represent the only contract-management process that proactively assists parties in a project to avoid or (if necessary) resolve disputes in a timely and cost-effective manner. DBs are an integral part of many major construction projects worldwide. In addition, other industries such as information technology, insurance, defense and manufacturing have begun to employ the DB process for large and complex contracts.

Role of the DRBF

In 1996, the DRBF was established as a non-profit organization by a group of professionals involved in construction dispute resolution. Their goal was to promote the use of the DB process and to serve as an educational resource and information exchange for owners, contractors and DB members. The first book on DBs, the "Construction Dispute Review Board Manual," written by DRBF founders Robert Matyas, Al Mathews, Bob Smith and Joe Sperry, was published that year by McGraw-Hill.

Since then, the DRBF has continuously worked to develop training programs and resources focused on best practices and ethical conduct in dispute resolution for projects. In 2001, the DRBF awarded the first "Al Mathews Award for Dispute Board Excellence," an honor now given annually for exemplary service in advancing the use of the DB process. In 2017, the DRBF introduced an "Excellence in Dispute Avoidance & Resolution Award," given annually to project teams using the DB process.

The DRBF project database has tracked the use of DBs on projects worth in total more than US$275 billion worldwide. The DRBF has grown to an international membership approaching 1,000 and is represented in more than 70 countries. Each year, the DRBF hosts educational seminars and conferences and publishes updated materials on the evolution of the DB process.

Chapter 2
The Case for Dispute Boards

Over the years, owners and contractors involved in major projects have resolved their contractual disputes using a variety of methods that range from court litigation to alternative dispute resolution (ADR) processes such as arbitration, mediation and adjudication. One of the more recent and successful developments in the ADR space is the introduction of Dispute Boards (DBs) into the contract and dispute-management process.

DBs are an important aspect of best-practice project management. Major projects, particularly those within the construction industry, give rise to significant levels of participant risk, depending upon project type, complexity, duration and available budget.

Risk Management

As part of the design and procurement for a project, an owner typically will carry out a comprehensive risk review and develop a risk-management plan to handle and mitigate identifiable risks. Project management tools are then used to manage that risk.

For example, optimizing risk allocation in contracts seeks to put the risk on the party best able to avoid, mitigate or absorb liability. Certain defined risks can also be covered by insurance, and other risks are addressed within contract management processes, such as safety and quality assurance programs.

The primary types of risk that DBs address involve project cost and time. When cost and time issues arise within a project (as they inevitably do), and the contracting parties disagree about their responsibility for these risks, a DB is able to advise, assist and resolve the issues.

In its dispute avoidance role, the DB assists the parties in managing or resolving contentious issues and contractual disagreements before they develop into a formal dispute. In its dispute resolution role, the DB provides the parties with an independent recommendation or decision on formal disputes, thus enabling the parties to resolve such matters at the project level.

> **"DRBs have become quite common on very substantial infrastructure type projects around the world, many of them involving hundreds of millions of dollars or more... DRBs can look at disputes as they emerge and make recommendations to the parties with a view to 'nipping in the bud' such incipient disputes."**
>
> — Sir Robert Akenhead, International Arbitrator and former Judge of the UK High Court

Dispute Management

From a business perspective, conventional dispute management and resolution can be very costly. Not only are there significant additional costs in hiring expert consultants and lawyers, but project personnel can become tied up in preparing or defending claims rather than focusing on delivering the project.

In addition, unresolved and protracted disputes can lead to delays and disruption to work on the project, increasing costs and causing a breakdown of relationships and communications. With public/ government projects, such disputes can also generate community and political issues (and additional costs and delays) that may have an impact well beyond the confines of the project.

Finally, unresolved disputes lingering after the end of the project can cause parties to become entrenched in positions which often lead to months and years of extremely costly arbitration or litigation.

"The University of Washington has been using DRBs as its primary dispute resolution process for over 15 years. DRBs are integrated into the collaborative project teams as a 'Dispute Prevention Board.' Since starting our DRB process, UW has had no litigation and over the past 10 years has had no formal disputes or claims."

— Eric Smith, Director Major Projects Group Capital Projects Office, University of Washington

Dispute Boards as Project Insurance

Sometimes, owners and contractors only see DBs as an extra cost, rather than as a cost-effective management tool.

A comparison with project insurance is instructive in this regard. Owners and contractors, without hesitation, spend large sums of money on lines of insurance for projects: general liability, professional liability, workers compensation, builder's risk, umbrella policies, etc. Larger and more complex projects often implement owner- or contractor-controlled insurance programs which, in addition to actual policy costs, bring associated costs of managing and administering the program.

The purpose of these insurance programs is to prevent or minimize losses (the prevention function) and/or to pay for losses that may arise through a transfer of risk to insurers (the resolution function). These functions are

"The DRB process appears to be effective in assisting in the resolution of disputes, leading to more timely completion of projects, reduced cost overruns and avoidance of claims. Utilization of DRBs on larger projects can serve to motivate greater cooperation between parties resulting in fewer unresolved claims and a reduced litigation potential."

— Florida Department of Transportation, Office of Inspector General similar to the role of a DB, although a DB serves a much wider and more positive purpose in influencing project outcomes.

An insurance program is deemed a success if it serves to prevent losses, and the insurance coverage resolves losses that occur during the project. The fact that millions of dollars in insurance premiums and administrative costs are invested to prevent and resolve losses is deemed to be a wise expenditure because it mitigated and absorbed the project risks. Yet, statistics collected by the DRBF indicate the cost of insurance on major projects almost always exceeds the cost of a DB by a significant margin, even before accounting for other benefits of a DB.

Cost-Benefit Analysis

A cost-benefit analysis for the use of DBs on a project begins by weighing the relatively fixed costs of a DB (see Chapter 11) against the benefits realized by minimizing the cost/time impact of disputed issues. There are a number of important factors to consider:

- The carrying costs of a DB relative to the budget of the project are small, usually in the range of 0.05 percent to 0.15 percent of project costs.
- A DB works within the management structure of the project to minimize project costs. For example, the DB will often attend senior management meetings held in conjunction with DB meetings. The DB can also schedule on-site meetings convenient to the parties that are directed at optimizing project outcomes.
- The extra marginal cost of a DB is less than any other formal dispute resolution process. The DB is relatively informal, often does not involve external consultants or lawyers, does not include any document-discovery procedure and uses real-time information readily available to both the parties and the DB.
- Comparison studies between non-DB projects and DB projects almost always demonstrate positive outcomes. DB projects, as compared to non-DB projects, have significantly fewer and smaller cost overruns and schedule delays.

In short, the cost of a DB will deliver a positive return on investment as a result of faster project-delivery times, the minimization of cost overruns, the prevention of most disputes and a much lower cost of resolution for unavoidable disputes.

Florida DOT: DB Contracts Outshine Others
One-Year Study by Florida Department of Transportation in 2013

Number of Contracts   ●Time Overrun   ●Cost Overrun

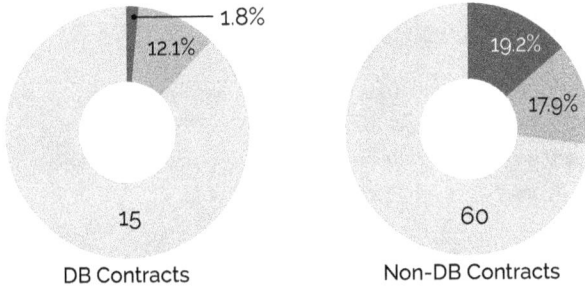

1.8%
12.1%

19.2%

17.9%

15

60

DB Contracts

Non-DB Contracts

Contracts lasting longer than 1 year

Other Dispute Board Benefits

DBs also provide other important "soft" benefits to a project. Regular DB meetings with project teams promote open communication and collaborative behavior that help preserve contractual relationships. DBs encourage the parties to address problems that could result in disputes at an early stage, when they are most amenable to resolution. DBs also can act to facilitate best-for-project solutions that minimize cost and time overruns.

Even when disputes do arise, the DB hearing process provides a way to channel and manage conflict in an orderly and neutral manner. The DB process is the only alternative dispute-resolution process that happens in real time. Disputes can be quickly resolved while the project is proceeding, thus allowing management to focus on the delivery of better project outcomes. In addition, outcomes of the DB process respect and maintain the contract provisions and the allocation of risk because the DB is required to apply contract terms as agreed in the contract documents.

Finally, DBs provide a dispute resolution process with integrity and procedural fairness. The DB process is based on factual records, project documentation and applicable law. The DB will provide reasoned and detailed findings by experienced and independent experts who understand the project, the players and the facts of the dispute. The DB provides both owners and contractors a merit-based process in which they can have utmost confidence.

2018 Study: Dispute Boards Avoid, Limit Disputes

The Asian Development Bank (ADB) asked the DRBF to evaluate the effectiveness of DBs and make recommendations on implementation for projects financed by ADB. The DRBF study covered more than 230 projects.

The study results demonstrate:
- A strong preference for standing DBs over ad hoc DBs.
- An overwhelming preference (95%) for DBs to adopt dispute avoidance processes.
- When dispute avoidance is practiced, the probability of an issue ending up in arbitration is very low (6%).
- Of 337 DB advisory opinions, only 7% went on to a formal DB referral requiring a recommendation or decision.
- Of 512 DB decisions, only 6% were referred to arbitration and only seven of those decisions were ultimately overturned.
- The DB process had a success rate of 94% in avoiding expensive follow-on dispute resolution procedures.

Chapter 3
Dispute Boards and Other ADR Processes

Alternative Dispute Resolution (ADR) typically refers to alternatives to court-based litigation. DBs are seen as a type of ADR process in every legal jurisdiction in which they are utilized. This chapter offers a comparison of DBs to three other common ADR processes — mediation, expert determination/ adjudication and arbitration.

In general, DBs differ from other ADR processes in that a DB is the only process that enables parties to engage in dispute prevention as well as dispute resolution. As discussed in more detail in Chapter 13, a DB performs its dispute prevention role by periodically meeting with the parties to address and head off issues that might result in disputes. The DB is also available to provide advisory opinions on issues when the parties are unable to reach agreement. This usually enables the parties to resolve issues before they become formal disputes.

As discussed in more detail in Chapters 14 to 16, a DB performs its dispute resolution role by conducting informal hearings and providing the parties with reasoned recommendations or decisions related to their disputes. None of the other ADR processes combine both the dispute avoidance and dispute resolution functions.

DBs also differ from other ADR processes because the DB is typically appointed at the start of the project and engaged until completion. This allows DB members to develop a relationship built on confidence and trust with the parties, increasing the likelihood of the parties accepting the DB's advisory opinions and decisions if formal disputes arise.

The DB also acquires detailed knowledge and information about the project because it is aware of events and actions as they unfold. Site visits and meetings provide ready access to the personnel doing the work. In comparison with the other ADR processes, this active involvement gives the DB a deeper and more accurate understanding of the parties' positions as well as the facts and circumstances surrounding any particular dispute.

The following sections provide a summary of the similarities and differences between DBs and the other ADR processes.

Mediation

Mediation typically involves engaging an experienced, independent mediator to assist the parties in reaching a settlement on a dispute or disputes that the parties have been unable to resolve between themselves. The key similarities and differences to DBs are:

Similarities
- A mediator will often have expertise in the subject matter of the dispute.
- Both processes are collaborative, in the sense that the parties are seeking to resolve their dispute amicably on agreed terms.
- The costs of preparing for and conducting a mediation are comparable to a DB hearing.

Differences
- A mediator has no role in dispute prevention, since he/she is only appointed after a formal dispute arises.
- Mediation is not conducted in real time but rather after the event, when positions have hardened and best-for-project outcomes may not be possible.
- Typically, the mediation process is controlled by lawyers rather than project personnel and is likely to be adversarial since parties usually stake out an extreme position from which to negotiate.

- A mediator has no prior knowledge about project details or evolution of the dispute.
- A mediated outcome generally does not facilitate or inform the parties' future contract performance.

Expert Determination (Adjudication)

Expert determination (often referred to as "adjudication" in some legal systems) involves bringing in an independent third party to make a quick "merits" determination of the issues in dispute.

The parties are usually bound to give immediate effect to the decision; although, the decision may not be final and binding if subsequent arbitration is permitted. It is reviewable by a court only on a narrow set of issues.

Adjudication typically is statutory based, giving little or no flexibility for the parties to adjust the process to suit the dispute in question. Expert determination usually is contractually based, giving more flexibility for the parties to tailor the process to the particular type of dispute and the nature of the project. The key similarities and differences to DBs are:

Similarities
- The independent expert has expertise in the subject matter of the dispute.
- The process can be conducted expeditiously during the project but may not be in real time, depending on when the dispute is referred to the expert.

Differences
- The expert has no role in dispute prevention, since he/she is only appointed to deal with formal disputes.

- The lack of participation by personnel involved during the project means the expert is not well informed about the project or underlying facts of the dispute.
- The involvement of lawyers and consultants usually results in a more adversarial process and significantly greater costs.
- The process is not collaborative and does not assist in maintaining project relationships.

Arbitration

Arbitration involves appointing an independent third party or a three-person tribunal to conduct a formal hearing of the dispute.

Arbitration has many of the hallmarks of a court process since the parties' cases are presented by lawyers following courtroom procedures.

Frequently, the arbitrator is a lawyer. The arbitrator will issue a reasoned decision ("an award"), which is immediately binding on the parties.

In most jurisdictions, arbitration has statutory underpinnings, but parties may specify contractually their own procedural rules or adopt those of an arbitral institution, such as the International Chamber of Commerce (ICC). Parties usually have a right to appeal arbitration awards in court but only on narrow grounds. The key similarities and differences with DBs are:

Similarities
- An arbitrator usually has expertise in the subject matter of the dispute.
- An arbitrator's award is based on the terms of the contract, the applicable law and the merits of the dispute.

Differences

- An arbitrator has no role in dispute prevention, since he/she is only appointed to hear and determine formal disputes.
- An arbitrator is not well informed about project details or the background to the dispute, except for submissions and evidence put forward during the hearing that relate only to issues in dispute.
- There is usually heavy involvement of lawyers and expert consultants in the arbitration process, resulting in high costs and lengthy delays in resolution.
- The arbitration process has many similarities to litigation. For example, procedural rules may allow "discovery" of documents, interlocutory and dispositive applications, memorials or statements of evidence on oath, formal hearings with oral testimony and cross-examination, and a transcript or record of the proceedings.

A Comparison of Alternative Dispute Resolution Processes

	Dispute Board	Mediation/Facilitation
Personnel required	1 or 3 DB member(s)	1 mediator/facilitator
How appointed?	Selection by parties	Selection by parties
When is the process implemented?	Start of project	After dispute arises
Speed of process	Quick, real-time	Variable, can be quick
Nature of process	Pro-active for all issues and interactive	Reactive to dispute only but still interactive
Time at which disputes are addressed	As they occur. Often issues are resolved before they become disputes.	During the project
Effect on parties' relationships	Maintains relationships	Assists in maintaining relationships
Amount of time and effort required from parties	Low to medium but with regular commitment	Low to medium but usually one-off
Relative cost	Low	Low/medium
Dispute avoidance	Only process which is directed at avoiding disputes	None
Dispute resolution	Provides recommendations or binding decisions	Provides options for settlement
Rules governing the process	Specified in contract or institutional rules	As agreed between parties and mediator/facilitator

Expert Determination /Adjudication	Arbitration
1 expert/adjudicator	1 or 3 arbitrator(s)
Selection by parties	Selection by parties or third-party nomination
After dispute arises	Usually at/after project completion
Variable, can be prolonged	Lengthy and slow
Reactive to dispute only	Reactive to disputes only and similar to formal litigation
During or at end of project	Usually at end of project
Adversarial - does not assist in maintaining relationships	Adversarial – destroys relationships
Medium to high but usually one-off	High, with long-term commitment
Medium	Very high
None	None
Binding decision	Final and binding decisions
May be specified in contract. Often governed by institutional rules	Statutory and/or institutional rules

2

Dispute Board Concepts

Chapter 4
The Dispute Board Process

Although the DB process is relatively new as a dispute resolution approach for major projects (see Chapter 1), it has proven to be remarkably successful. The distinguishing feature of the DB process is clear from many years of use. If employed properly, the DB process can provide a low cost and highly effective means of assisting parties in a project — not only to resolve disputes quickly, but more importantly, to avoid disputes and achieve optimum project outcomes.

Defining the Board

A DB typically consists of three members. Some DBs, however, may have only a single member (see Chapter 7).

A DB member is a respected and trusted professional who is selected for his/her knowledge, experience and independence in the subject matter of the project (see Chapter 5). Typically for a construction project, a DB may include a mix of engineers, contractors, architects, builders, consultants and lawyers, all of whom are specialists in construction work. All DB members must be approved by the contracting parties. DB members must remain independent and impartial at all times, and do not represent a specific contracting party.

The Dispute Board's Role

The DB meets with the parties regularly during the project and helps them to avoid and, if necessary, resolve issues and disputes. The DB does this by providing an impartial forum for resolution of disputes in real time and at minimal cost.

The very existence of a readily available dispute-avoidance and resolution process which draws on mutually selected, technically knowledgeable and experienced "neutrals" familiar with the project, fosters agreement on problems that might otherwise be subject to lengthy and costly arbitration or litigation.

How Dispute Boards Operate

The DB is normally formed when the parties enter into a contract for delivery of the project. At that time, the parties also enter into a formal DB Agreement with each of the DB members. However, a DB may be established at any time if the parties agree.

The DB Agreement sets out the parties' respective responsibilities as well as the functions and obligations of the DB. Costs of the DB are usually shared equally between the owner and the contractor.

Meetings between the contracting parties and the DB are typically held at the project site at regular intervals and will often include a site inspection. At the meetings, which are attended by both off-site executives and senior on-site personnel, the DB receives an update on the progress of all aspects of the project. The DB is informed about issues that could cause cost increases or delays and is also informed about any unresolved issues that could become disputes. The DB discusses and consults with the parties on ways and means to resolve the issues.

Between regular DB meetings, the DB is kept apprised of progress through monthly reports, minutes of meetings and other documentation the parties and/or the DB consider necessary to keep the DB properly informed at all times.

If any issue arising under the contract remains unresolved after negotiations between the parties and discussions with the DB, then either party may formally refer that dispute to the DB for a recommendation or decision.

Constituting a Dispute Board

Selection processes vary, and there are several common methods in practice. The owner and contractor both need to identify preferred DB nominees, taking into consideration qualifications, availability, experience and background (see Chapter 5 and Chapter 12).

Nominees may be required to provide a formal declaration as to impartiality and independence from parties or persons associated with the project. Once the DB nominees have been approved by the parties, the DB is formally established by the parties and the DB members jointly executing a DB Agreement.

What Makes Dispute Boards Effective?

Most construction contracts without a DB specify a strict dispute-resolution process that must be followed if a dispute occurs. In contrast, the DB's dispute avoidance role is not confined to any predetermined process. This allows the DB to engage the parties in dispute-avoidance strategies best suited to resolve an issue at hand.

By constituting the DB as soon as possible after the contract is executed, the DB becomes familiar with the project from the start, when issues may arise and disputes can develop. The early establishment of a DB also commits the parties to a framework intended to resolve issues and avoid disputes by encouraging positive relationships and open communication between the parties at all levels.

As the DB monitors and is updated on progress of the work and any ongoing issues between the parties, the DB is ready and able to assist the parties in addressing issues in real time as they occur. Early resolution of issues before they become disputes preserves relationships and greatly reduces both costs and the loss of productive project time.

The presence of senior off-site personnel at DB meetings not only keeps them better apprised about progress at the project site, it also allows them the opportunity to use their authority to intervene in heading off potential disputes.

However, if the parties cannot resolve an issue and it becomes a dispute, the DB can resolve it within a short period of time, once a formal referral has been made by one of the parties. When a dispute is referred to the DB for resolution, the DB process is cost-effective when compared with other methods of dispute resolution (see Chapter 3).

Dispute Avoidance

The DB has a wide range of dispute-avoidance techniques it may use depending on the issue (see Chapter 13).

Typically, the DB takes a proactive stance and encourages dispute avoidance by addressing project management and resolution of issues during regular DB meetings. The DB routinely inquires about potential issues, claims or disputes, and reviews and monitors the status of such matters with the parties. The DB also urges the parties to discuss early resolution of issues and to use the DB to facilitate informal sessions or special meetings with the parties or interested third parties.

Knowing a dispute may be referred to the DB for resolution encourages the parties to resolve issues that could become disputes. DB feedback to the parties causes them to critically assess their respective positions on the issue at hand.

Furthermore, before formally referring a dispute to the DB, the parties may seek an informal, nonbinding advisory opinion from the DB. The benefit of such an advisory opinion is it can often be provided by the DB on short notice and commonly results in the resolution of an issue that otherwise may have been formally referred to the DB for a recommendation or decision.

Dispute Resolution

When the parties cannot resolve disputes in a timely manner, either by themselves or with the assistance of the DB, either party may formally refer the dispute to the DB (see Chapter 14).

Typically, the DB Agreement governs the process that leads to delivery of a recommendation or decision. This usually involves each party providing position papers, documents and evidence related to the dispute, with each party then given the opportunity to respond to the other party's submissions (see Chapter 15).

A hearing/conference is held by agreement of the parties, or when the DB requires it from the parties. This allows the parties to further explain their respective positions and to respond to the other side's case. Lawyers may or may not be permitted during such hearings, depending on the DB Agreement (see Chapter 16).

Following the presentation and submission of all relevant material, the DB then produces a written recommendation or decision — which includes the DB's analysis and reasoning — within the time frame required by the DB Agreement (see Chapter 17).

Depending on the form and provisions of the contract, the DB may issue a nonbinding recommendation or a binding decision (subject only to later arbitration). In either case, experience has shown that the provision of a well-reasoned analysis of the dispute by a panel of neutral, highly experienced professionals almost invariably results in settlement of the dispute without subsequent legal proceedings.

Chapter 5
Qualities and Attributes of Dispute Board Members

Requirements for establishing a DB for a project are generally set out within the dispute resolution clauses of the contract between the parties and in the DB Agreement. In all such provisions, the selection and appointment of DB members with appropriate skills and experience is fundamental to the success of the DB process. This chapter outlines the qualities and attributes required of those who wish to serve as a member of a DB.

Impartiality and Independence

To ensure success of the DB process and to be a successful DB member, there is an absolute requirement to be impartial and independent at all times.

DB members need to gain and retain the trust and confidence of the parties to the contract. The building and maintenance of that trust is the key to the successful operation of a DB. The relationship between the DB and the parties must be based on open and full disclosure and the maintenance of impartiality and independence by all DB members.

Although a DB member may be nominated by one of the parties to the contract, it is fundamental that a DB member does not act, at any time, as an advocate or representative of either party. The DB member, after appointment, must act in the interests of the project as a whole and must always be seen to be impartial and independent in all respects.

The concepts of impartiality and independence are well established in most legal systems and jurisdictions. According to common definitions:

- **Impartiality** means *having no direct involvement or interest and not favoring one person or side more than another.*

- **Independence** means *free from the influence, control or determination of another or others.*

These definitions are complementary and largely self-explanatory. Impartiality and independence are at the core of the DRBF's Code of Ethical Conduct (see Chapter 6).

The question of whether a DB nominee or DB member is impartial must be considered, not only with regard to evidence of actual bias but to the idea of a perception of bias. In legal terminology, the test for bias is *whether a fair-minded and independent observer, having considered the background, experience and behavior of the DB nominee/member, might conclude that a real possibility of bias exists.*

However, questions of impartiality and the perception of bias are often subjective matters. A proper assessment of impartiality should be made by the parties in each case, prior to nominating a DB member. In addition, in performing the role, the DB member must continue to act impartially throughout the duration of the DB.

In contrast to impartiality, independence is largely based on objective facts and can be assessed from information disclosed by the DB nominee (see Chapter 12). For example, if a financial tie exists between one of the parties and the DB nominee, then that nominee clearly is not independent. Other examples of a lack of independence include a prior involvement in the project or a close relationship with a party representative.

DB nominees must be independent of the parties at the time of accepting an appointment to serve as a DB member and must remain so until the appointment is terminated. This means that a DB member's role on the DB will preclude any other relationship with the parties or with other entities involved with the project.

Conflicts of Interest

The concept of a "conflict of interest" is a narrower and more specific version of the general concept of impartiality and independence. As part of the requirement for impartiality and independence, DB members must be free from conflicts of interest at all times.

In simple terms, a conflict of interest is a conflict between the competing interests of someone in a decision-making position, here a DB member. A simple example is that an employee of a company could not act as an independent expert, mediator or arbitrator in a dispute involving his or her employer because of the obvious two conflicting interests involved.

A conflict of interest with respect to a DB member cannot be viewed solely on the basis of a strict legal test but needs to be addressed in the broader context of what might be considered to be a "commercial" conflict or the appearance of such a conflict. The ethical implications of a conflict of interest are also important (see Chapter 6). In the context of a DB, a conflict of interest will arise if a prospective DB member falls within any of the following criteria:

- *Has a financial interest in the contract or the project or a financial interest in a party directly involved in the project.* A financial interest includes, for example, the beneficial ownership of shares in a party, whether held personally or in other legal arrangements such as trusts, partnerships or investment funds. A DB member should not benefit, however indirectly, from service on a DB except by payments received for services rendered under the DB Agreement.

- *Does not disclose to the contracting parties prior to appointment to the DB, all current and previous employment by, or financial ties to, any party directly involved in the project.* Previous employment or financial ties within a specified time period will normally preclude serving on the DB. A typical time period is two years, but longer qualifying periods may be mandated in some circumstances. Previous and current roles as a DB member, a mediator, arbitrator, etc., relating to other contracts involving one or more of the same parties (or an entity controlled by one of the parties) must also be disclosed. Full disclosure in advance of a DB appointment will ensure that each party can assess and be satisfied that such past or present relationships will not affect the independence and impartiality of the DB member.

- *Does not disclose to the contracting parties prior to appointment to the DB any current or previous close professional, social or personal relationship with a director, officer or employee of any party directly involved in the project.* Such relationships frequently form in the working environment and where there are common interests in community associations, or social, religious or sporting organizations. Persons with the depth of experience necessary for DB service are often likely to have had previous professional contact with one or more of the parties' representatives. While such relationships will not preclude serving on the DB, disclosure ensures all parties are aware of any non-financial relationships that might be perceived as affecting the impartiality or independence of the DB.

- *Does not disclose a separate fiduciary relationship (for example, as an employee or consultant) with any party involved in the contract.* In this regard, the consent of the contracting parties should also be obtained before serving as a DB member on another project that involves one of the same parties.

- *Does not disclose to the contracting parties any fact or circumstance that arises that could reasonably be considered by a contracting party as likely to affect the DB member's ongoing independence or impartiality.* This obligation continues throughout the term of the DB.

- *Has multiple past or present appointments as a DB member by one of the contracting parties.* Several DB nominations and appointments by the same party may give rise to a reasonable concern about partiality or bias, at least in the eyes of an objective observer.

It is the parties to the contract, not the prospective DB member, who must determine whether a conflict of interest exists. The prospective DB member must make a full disclosure of past and present associations and interests to allow the parties to make a fully informed decision (see Chapter 12).

Following the disclosure by a DB nominee or DB member of an actual or potential conflict of interest, he or she must decline the nomination or resign from the DB, if requested by both contracting parties.

However, if such a request is made by only one party, the DB member's position should be considered and discussed with both parties and the other members of the DB. If the declared conflict is remote or inconsequential and the DB member confirms that he/she is and will remain independent and impartial, the contracting parties are likely to agree to the appointment or retention of the DB member.

Selection of Dispute Board Members

To ensure the DB is constituted as a suitable and appropriately qualified team, the parties to a contract need to consider a variety of criteria when choosing DB members. These criteria range from skills and experience to availability, impartiality and independence.

When the contracting parties appoint a DB member, the prospective DB member's qualifications and attributes relevant to the project must be considered, as well as any criteria set by the parties or any requirements noted in the parties' contract. For multi-national contracts, nationality and relevant language skills will be significant. For many projects, the inclusion of a lawyer and/or an experienced dispute resolution specialist as a member of the DB will also be an important consideration.

Where the DB member being selected is to fill the role of DB Chair, additional criteria are usually applicable (see below).

Qualifications and Experience

Ideally, DB members should be experienced in a range of technical, contractual, and commercial matters relevant to the project. Experience-related criteria that should be considered include:

- Experience in the type of work and risks involved in the project, especially if the work is of a specialized nature (for example, tunneling or telecommunications).
- General management and commercial experience on major projects.
- Dispute resolution experience (for example as a facilitator, mediator, expert or arbitrator).
- Experience in relevant legal matters, especially the interpretation of contracts and technical specifications.
- Familiarity with the delivery method for the project (for example, design-build, PPP, etc.).
- Prior training and experience as a DB member.

Attributes

DB members must have good management and communication skills and be fluent in the relevant language for communications. Attributes that should be considered include:

- Training in and an understanding of the DB role and process.
- Strong people skills for effective communication and negotiation.
- Skill and experience in the effective conduct of meetings.
- Experience in the procedural aspects of dispute resolution processes and the conduct of hearings.
- The ability to write reports, recommendations, and reasoned decisions in a concise and logical manner.
- Possession of skills complementary to the other DB members and appropriate for the type of project and its delivery method.

Availability

DB members should ensure they will be available for all site visits and regular DB meetings for the duration of the project. If a DB nominee has schedule constraints, these should be made known to the parties at the time of nomination.

Specific issues related to availability that should be addressed by a potential DB member include:

- Being overcommitted on other work and therefore not available for regular DB meetings or site visits in a timely manner.
- Being reasonably available at short notice to deal promptly with issues or disputes that may arise.
- Being able to prepare and issue written advisory opinions, recommendations and/or decisions to the parties in a timely manner.
- Being in reasonable physical health to perform the requirements of the DB role for the duration of the project.

Dispute Board Chair – Qualifications and Experience

A DB Chair is required to perform a variety of additional tasks, including:

- Assuming a greater share of the DB workload. The Chair is required to act as the primary administrative interface between the DB and the contracting parties.
- Managing the DB process, such as setting schedules and agendas, chairing regular DB meetings and hearings, arranging site inspections and communicating with the parties.
- Facilitating open and informal discussions between DB members and party representatives.
- Coordinating the preparation of the DB's advisory opinions, recommendations and/or decisions.
- Preparing and/or approving the notes of DB meetings prior to distribution to the parties.
- Meeting with the contracting parties' senior executives from time to time.

The Chair should be chosen primarily for his or her experience in managing the DB process. The ability to effectively integrate the DB within the senior management structure of the project is also important. Similar to the attributes required of a DB member (see above), the desirable attributes of a DB Chair include:

- Experience and familiarity with the DB process and the role of the DB in regular meetings, in the advisory process and in DB hearings.
- Availability and willingness to handle the administrative aspects of the DB workload (for example, communications with the parties, scheduling, etc.).
- Prior training (for example, attendance at a DRBF Chairing workshop).
- Good communication and facilitation skills that encourage open and informal discussion.
- Having a good reputation and respect within one's profession in order to help obtain and retain the confidence of the parties and the other DB members.

Some DB Agreements allow for Chair rotation from time to time among the DB members, but this is uncommon in practice. In the case of a one-person DB, the DB member should possess the qualifications and experience of a Chair (as noted above).

Chapter 6

DRBF Code of Ethical Conduct

The independent and impartial role of a DB makes it essential that Board members act in a highly ethical manner. Every member must not only be independent of the contracting parties and any related entity, but should act in a manner that is, and is perceived to be, neutral and impartial at all times. For a DB to function effectively, DB members must establish and maintain good working relationships based on trust and integrity, both among fellow DB members and with the contracting parties.

To this end, DRBF has established a Code of Ethical Conduct, which sets out the key aspects of personal and professional conduct to which each DB member should subscribe. The Code comprises four Canons of Ethics, to be observed throughout the DB process. Contracting parties are encouraged to include compliance with the DRBF Code as an obligation in their DB Agreement.

An explanation of the required ethical conduct underlying each Canon and some practical guidelines to assist DB members in complying with the Code, are set out below. In the Code language below, DB members are referred to as Board members.

Canon 1 – Conflict of Interest and Disclosure

Board members must avoid any actual or potential conflict of interest during the term of the Dispute Board. Board members must disclose, before their appointment, any interest, past or present relationship, or association that could reasonably be considered by a contracting party as likely to affect that member's independence or impartiality. If, during the term of the Dispute Board, a Board member becomes aware of any fact or circumstance that might reasonably be considered by a contracting party as likely to affect that Board member's independence or impartiality, the Board member must inform the other Board members and disclose the matter to the contracting parties.

To protect the credibility and integrity of the DB, Board members must disclose any interests or relationships that may affect their independence or impartiality or create an appearance of partiality or bias. As a general principle, if there is any doubt as to whether a DB member should disclose certain facts or circumstances, the question should be resolved in favor of disclosure. The potential conflicts of interest that would prevent a DB member from complying with Canon 1 of the DRBF Code are set out in Chapter 5.

If a conflict of interest exists, a DB nominee should decline his/her appointment to the DB. If a conflict arises after appointment (for example, due to an acquisition or merger by one of the parties), a DB member should make an appropriate disclosure (see Chapter 12) at the earliest opportunity. After consideration of the circumstances of the conflict by the other DB members and the contracting parties, the DB member may be asked to resign or should do so at his or her own volition.

Canon 2 – Confidentiality

Board members must ensure that information acquired during the term of the Dispute Board remains confidential and must not be disclosed, unless such information is already in the public domain. Any such confidential information may only be disclosed if approved by the contracting parties or if compelled by law. Board members must not use such confidential information for any purpose beyond the activities of the Dispute Board.

Establishing trust and confidence with the contracting parties is of paramount importance in the DB process. The DB Agreement will generally impose confidentiality obligations that must be respected by each DB member.

When carrying out its dispute avoidance and prevention activities (see Chapter 13), the DB must ensure it provides a confidential and informal environment in which the contracting parties are encouraged to discuss and resolve issues before they become disputes.

If the DB is operating in a common law jurisdiction, the legal concept of "without prejudice" is often applied to oral and written communications within the DB process. Without prejudice means the parties are free to discuss issues, make concessions and explore possible solutions, safe in the knowledge that if the matter in question is not resolved and later becomes a formal dispute, those discussions and concessions cannot be raised and used against them.

Information disclosed to the DB should remain confidential. DB members must respect this confidentiality and treat the contract and any other details of the project, as well as their own activities — which are clearly not public knowledge — as confidential to the DB process. A DB member must not make any disclosures, oral or written, of such information without the prior written permission of the parties. Information gained by a DB member during the DB process must not be used or passed on to others for personal advantage or other purposes.

If and when disputes arise, the DB process provides a private and confidential means for the parties to resolve their contractual issues. The parties' documentary records and submissions in relation to a dispute, as well as the DB's findings, reports, recommendations and decisions, will generally not be available in the public arena, except strictly as agreed to by the contracting parties or as required by law (for example, by statute in some states or in court proceedings).

The reporting (to the DRBF or other professional bodies) of statistical and factual data (often in redacted form) relating to a DB or a listing of the project in a DB member's resume or curriculum vitae, is generally not regarded as a breach of confidentiality. However, it is recommended that DB members should obtain prior approval from the contracting parties.

Canon 3 – Board Conduct and Communications

Board members must conduct all Board activities in an expeditious, diligent, orderly and impartial manner. Board members must act honestly, with integrity and without bias. There must be no unilateral communications between a Board member and a contracting party, except as permitted under the Dispute Board operating procedures or as agreed between the parties.

The contracting parties are entitled to expect that DB proceedings will be conducted in an expeditious, diligent, orderly and impartial manner. The DB Chair, or (where appropriate) the sole DB member, must ensure that meetings are conducted on a business-like basis and in accordance with applicable contract requirements, the DB Agreement, and the operating procedures adopted.

The DB should follow 'best practice' meeting procedures such as issuing agendas and meeting summaries, site visit reports, action lists, and the like. The hearing process (see details under Canon 4) should also be managed expeditiously and impartially, while still ensuring a fair process for all parties.

Communication protocols are important and must be followed. All communications with the DB should be sent to all DB members. DB members must avoid any unilateral (ex parte) communications with a contracting party.

All communications from the DB to the contracting parties should be through the DB Chair (with the exception of certain administrative matters, such as DB members' fee invoices). The DB Chair must establish clear lines of communications by identifying points of contact with the contracting parties, with the understanding that these points of contact will forward DB communications internally as required within their respective organizations.

In both oral and written communications with the contracting parties, DB members must avoid giving any appearance of partiality or bias. An even-handed approach is essential. DB members must be sensitive to the possibility that pointed questions or negative comments, if poorly considered, may be misconstrued by a party as an indication of that DB member's partiality or bias (see Chapter 5).

Examples of improper and unethical conduct by DB members include:

- Private meetings or other communications with only one of the contracting parties.

- Making gratuitous or derogatory comments with respect to the project, the terms of the contract or the actions/inactions of a contracting party.
- Public criticism or disparagement of any individual, party, or DB member.
- Prejudging the merits of an issue without giving each party an opportunity to present its case and reply to the other party's position.
- Offering legal or technical advice beyond the DB member's defined role or expertise.
- Ignoring or attempting to rewrite the terms of the parties' contractual arrangements.
- Failure to respect an individual's cultural background, language, educational or professional experience.
- Acceptance of invitations, gifts or inducements from a contracting party, even if offered innocently and in good faith.
- Invoicing the contracting parties in a manner (or for an amount) that varies from that agreed to under the DB Agreement.

Canon 4 – Board Procedures

All Board meetings and hearings must be conducted in accordance with the applicable contract provisions and operating procedures, in a manner that provides procedural fairness to the contracting parties. Dispute Board recommendations and decisions must be made expeditiously on the basis of the provisions of the contract, the applicable law and the information, facts and circumstances submitted by the contracting parties.

Timely and impartial recommendations or decisions are important to the DB process. In considering disputes referred to it, the DB should implement a procedurally fair process that is timely and cost-effective.

Procedural fairness requires that the contracting parties receive a proper opportunity to prepare and present their submissions and all relevant information to the DB. A party must also be given the opportunity to answer submissions and information put before the DB by the other party. In this regard, DB members should act impartially at all times and without favor to either party. DB members must ensure that any dispute resolution process adopted by the DB meets these fundamental requirements, as well as complying with the DB Agreement and applicable operating procedures (see Chapters 15 and 16).

The DB's recommendations or decisions must be based on the specific provisions of the contract documents, applicable law of the relevant state or country, and information, facts and circumstances as submitted by the contracting parties. While DB members should apply their own expertise and experience to the resolution of any dispute, the DB must construe the contract objectively and not attempt to "rewrite" the terms because of perceived unfairness or unsuitability. Further, the DB must not ignore the requirements of applicable laws or statutes (see Chapter 17).

The obligation to ensure that a DB's recommendations or decisions comply with applicable law does not mean a DB must necessarily include a lawyer. While it is often the case that a DB member will have legal qualifications, non-lawyer DB members simply need to inform themselves of the relevant law as the need arises. In most situations, the contracting parties will, on their own initiative or at the request of the DB, provide submissions to the DB on any contested legal issues.

There is no place in a DB opinion, recommendation, or decision for criticism of a contracting party's (or an individual's) actions, management style or approach to the administration of the contract. Such comments will only lead to a perception that the DB is biased against the recipient because of such criticism.

The DB's recommendations or decisions must be, and be seen to be, objective, impersonal and supported by clear and logical reasoning based on the information available to the DB, the terms of the contract and applicable law.

3

Establishing
Dispute Boards

Chapter 7
Types of Dispute Boards

Several models for the structure of a DB are in common practice worldwide. These DB models are distinguished by their primary role within a project (dispute avoidance or resolution, or both), the number of DB members (ones or threes), the duration of the DB (standing or ad hoc) and the nature of the rules or procedures under which the DB operates.

Most DB models incorporate attributes that maximize successful project outcomes — such as establishment of the DB at the start of a project, appropriate DB member selection and regular involvement of the DB in project management and governance.

However, some of the DB's value may be compromised if the proper model is not utilized. For example, selecting a one-person DB for perceived cost savings may compromise the DB's effectiveness in large and/or complex projects, which benefit from the diversity of experience achieved with a three-person DB.

Three-Person Dispute Board

The most common form of DB is the three-person model. DB members are selected by various methods (see Chapter 12) and approved by both the owner and contractor.

Benefits of a three-person DB over a one-person DB include:

- Likely to have greater and more diverse experiences to bring to the project.
- Advisory opinions, recommendations and/or decisions carry greater weight, especially if such opinions and decisions are unanimous.
- Greater capacity and effectiveness in both its avoidance and determinative roles.

- Greater responsiveness and flexibility, as it can still function if one or two members of the DB are temporarily unavailable.
- One or two of the DB members, rather than all three, can be assigned to deal with a particular task, such as facilitating an informal meeting, to assist the parties in resolving their disputes.

One-Person Dispute Board

This DB model has been operating successfully for several years in many countries, and its use is increasing.

A one-person DB is particularly suitable for smaller projects where the cost of a three-person DB cannot be justified. However, a one-person DB is only fully effective when an independent person with all the desired qualifications and experience (see Chapter 5) is available to act. In practice, the primary benefit of a one-person DB when compared with a three-person DB is cost savings (see Chapter 11).

Dispute Resolution Advisor

The concept of a Dispute Resolution Advisor (DRA) was first developed in Hong Kong more than two decades ago and has been successfully exported to several other countries.

A DRA is similar to a one-person, standing DB, set up in the conventional manner at the commencement of the project. However, instead of the DRA having the power to provide a decision or recommendation on the merit of a dispute, the DRA's role is primarily that of an independent and experienced consultant, identifying potential areas of dispute and ensuring issues that arise are addressed by the parties as soon as possible.

The DRA member's other primary role is to assist the parties in informally resolving any dispute. The DRA is expected to assist the parties by acting as a facilitator to achieve an amicable dispute settlement or in structuring a suitable formal dispute resolution mechanism.

Dispute Board Panels

For large and complex construction projects with multiple contracts or alternative delivery methods, the most cost-effective means of dispute avoidance and resolution may be to establish a DB panel.

The panel should be made up of experienced DB practitioners, from which individual DB members can be selected to work on specific contracts within the overall project. A DB panel member may be called upon to act as a facilitator, mediator or adjudicator, as appropriate, when a dispute arises.

Three examples illustrate the flexibility of this DB model. In one instance, at the start of construction of a large airport complex, a panel called a Disputes Review Group (DRG), made up of six members, was formed to cover all the major contracts (about 20) on the project. Members of the DRG were chosen specifically to provide the range of expertise considered necessary to comprehend and deal with technical and commercial aspects of any dispute likely to arise. When a dispute arose, either one or three of the DRG members was selected and rapidly deployed to deal with the dispute.

In a second example, on a large underground railway project, two DB panels were established: a technical panel of engineers (who dealt with technical and construction-related disputes) and a financial panel of accountants and bankers (who handled disputes concerning financial provisions of the funding and concession agreements). In this example, when a dispute arose, a one-person DB could be appointed from either panel or a three-person DB could be appointed with DB members selected from both panels.

In these two examples, the DB panels were focused on dispute resolution and, thus, were unable to bring the advantages of dispute avoidance to the project.

In a third example, dispute avoidance was a primary objective. A DB panel was established prior to the start of construction on a very large highway project that included more than 200 bridges. There were more than 10 separate major contract with DBs.

The DB panel was preselected by the owner and consisted solely of DB members experienced in particular aspects of the work in each contract. As each contractor was appointed, a DB panel member was selected to act as a standing, one-person DB for that particular portion of the project. An experienced DB Chair was also appointed by the owner and the construction manager to provide oversight and coordination of each of the one-person DBs, ensuring consistency in overall project management.

Ad Hoc Dispute Boards

In this model, the DB is not established until the project is significantly advanced, or even completed. This model is often implemented in an effort to reduce costs. However, the ad hoc DB sacrifices the significant advantage of regular meetings with the parties and site visits to the project, thereby enabling the DB to promptly assist the parties in avoiding disputes and/or settling them amicably.

The ad hoc DB also removes the DB members' opportunities to establish rapport and credibility with the parties, an important factor to facilitating dispute resolution. As a general rule, the DRBF does not recommend the use of ad hoc DBs.

FIDIC and ICC Dispute Boards

FIDIC

FIDIC contracts utilize certain types of DBs, such as DAB and DAAB, based on specific contractual provisions. See Chapter 9 for details.

ICC

ICC Rules give parties a choice between three sub-types of DBs — each of which is distinguished by the outcome that results from the formal referral of a dispute. The three sub-types are:

- A Dispute Adjudication Board (DAB) issues decisions that must be complied with immediately.
- A Dispute Review Board (DRB) issues recommendations not immediately binding on the parties. However, the recommendations become binding if no party objects within 30 days.
- A Combined Dispute Board (CDB) offers an intermediate solution between a DRB and a DAB. A CDB will generally issue recommendations. But it may also issue decisions if a party so requests or if the DB so decides on the basis of criteria set out in ICC Rules.

Chapter 8

Best Practice Guidelines for Contract Documents

This chapter is intended as a guide for key contractual documents used to establish and operate successful DBs.

Given that different forms of DB contract provisions exist widely throughout the world, this chapter focuses on general principles of "best practice" documentation for DB contracts.

For example, many international projects use the FIDIC forms of contract (see Chapter 9) which include provisions for the establishment of a DB, the terms and conditions required for a DB Agreement and procedural rules relating to the scope of the DB's role and authority.

Some project contracts may specify the use of institutional DB rules and procedures (such as those published by ICC, CIArb, etc.). Some owners, such as public transportation authorities that are major users of the DB process, have developed custom forms of DB contract documents to suit their own project governance arrangements.

In all cases, documentation for a project will include a Dispute Resolution Clause that establishes an overall dispute resolution regime, as well as the role and function of the DB within the project's governance structure.

Details of the DB process should be set forth in three related documents:
- DB Specification
- DB Agreement
- DB Rules/Operating Procedures

In many countries outside North America, the contents of the DB Specification are incorporated into either the DB Agreement or DB Rules/Operating Procedures. Best practices for the content of each of these documents, required to establish a DB within a project, are outlined in the following sections.

Dispute Resolution Clause

The Dispute Resolution (DR) Clause sets forth the process by which contractual claims and disputes are processed. There are different schools of thought on how detailed the DR Clause should be. Some prefer that the DR Clause be kept simple with relatively short time frames for each step, so that a claim or dispute can be resolved early or brought forward to the DB in real time.

Others prefer that the DR Clause acts as a filtering system — with multiple opportunities to resolve the claim or dispute at escalating levels of project management (including the DB in its advisory capacity), before it is formally referred to the DB for resolution. The latter process, with more steps, takes longer and requires more party resources but may ultimately result in fewer disputes between the parties ending up with the DB.

Regardless of the specific type of DR Clause within a project contract, it will generally include:

- Notice provisions specifying when and how notice of a potential claim or dispute is given.
- Claim substantiation provisions that require the claimant to provide specified details and supporting information related to its claim(s).
- A process for claim evaluation and negotiation, during which the parties make submissions and exchange information.
- A hold point for acceptance or rejection of the claim between the parties.
- In the instance of rejection, the process for further review and determination of the claim. This could include additional review steps at the project management level or a specified referral process to the DB.
- Timelines for all of the above.

Although drafting of DR Clauses is beyond the scope of this guide, an important note for DB practice is to be clear in the DR Clause exactly what must be done to trigger the DB process, what time limits apply to each step and how the DB process fits within the overall project dispute resolution system. Attention to these matters will minimize disputes over procedural issues.

Dispute Board Specification

The DB Specification sets out requirements for the DB process, including such elements as establishment of the DB, selection and appointment of DB members and responsibilities of DB members in both their dispute avoidance and dispute resolution roles.

The DB Specification should clearly delineate the accepted role and jurisdiction of the DB, in a manner that allows the DB to retain a flexible approach to both dispute avoidance and dispute resolution.

At the critical stage when issues arise or the parties are already in dispute, it is important that the DB has strong, clear authority with which to take a robust attitude toward both dispute avoidance and dispute resolution. In handling a dispute, the DB must be empowered to determine its own jurisdiction and to establish its own procedures.

Recommended provisions to be included in the DB Specification:
- The obligation on both parties to establish the DB.
- Composition of the DB, whether it is to be a one- or three-person DB.
- Required qualifications for DB members.
- Disclosure and conflict of interest requirements.
- The process by which the parties select, nominate, and appoint the DB members.
- An appointment mechanism in the event of any failure of the parties to appoint a DB member.
- The responsibility of DB members to adhere to the DRBF Code of Ethical Conduct.

- DB's role in dispute avoidance, such as attending regular project meetings and site visits, and the opportunity to give informal advice or opinions.
- DB's role (if any) in facilitating negotiations or mediating a settlement between the parties.
- DB's role in and process for receiving, dealing with and resolving any dispute referred for a recommendation or decision.
- The parties' responsibilities once a dispute recommendation or decision is made.
- The process for dealing with a dispute if a party remains dissatisfied after the conclusion of the DB process, with steps and timelines specified.

Dispute Board Agreement

The DB Agreement is a professional services agreement that establishes the role, authority and obligations of the DB members and the contracting parties (owner and contractor) by means of a separate three-party contractual agreement. It is usually a separate document executed by each of the DB members and by both parties prior to establishment of the DB and its start of operation.

Caution

It is recommended that DB members carefully read the proposed DB Agreement before signing it and bring to the attention of the parties any missing provisions, inconsistencies or ambiguities, so they can be corrected or clarified before execution. The same attention should be given to the proposed DB Specification and DB Rules/Operating Procedures, to ensure that all these documents are consistent and acceptable to the DB members.

Recommended provisions to be included in the DB Agreement:
- Preamble: a listing of the contracting parties and an outline of the purpose and application of the DB Agreement

- Obligations on all parties
  - Disclosure requirements
  - Avoidance of conflicts of interest
  - Confidentiality
  - Compliance with the DRBF Code of Ethical Conduct
  - DB communications
  - DB procedures
- Scope of the DB role
  - Purpose and authority of the DB
  - Cross-references to DB Specification and DB Rules/Operating Procedures
- Owner responsibilities
  - Owner support of the DB process, good faith and mutual cooperation
- Contractor responsibilities
  - Contractor support of the DB process, good faith and mutual cooperation
- Fees and expenses
  - Schedule of DB fees and disbursements
  - Invoicing arrangements
  - Responsibility for payment
- Term and termination
  - Effective term of the DB Agreement
  - Process for resignation, termination and replacement of the DB
- Legal/administrative provisions
  - DB members as independent contractors
  - Liability and indemnity of DB members
  - Applicable law
  - Notices/communications

Dispute Board Rules/Operating Procedures

The DB Rules/Operating Procedures set out rules and procedures that have been agreed to by the DB members and the parties. These rules and procedures often include such details as meeting arrangements, communication protocols, dispute avoidance techniques, the requirements for the conduct of a hearing and the DB's decision-making process and functions.

The rules and procedures should be consistent with associated DB documentation, such as the DR Clause, the DB Specification and the DB Agreement.

The rules and procedures also should be flexible so that they can be altered from time to time by agreement between the DB members and the parties to reflect specific needs and circumstances of the project. To maintain the intended flexibility, it is recommended that the rules and procedures be adopted informally by review and consensus between the DB and the parties, rather than incorporating them as a contract document.

Recommended provisions to be included in the DB Rules/Operating Procedures:
- General statement of purpose
  - Application of the rules and procedures
  - Relationship to the DB Agreement
- Project information to be made available to DB Members
  - A full set of project documents
  - Timely transmittal of high-level information (monthly reports, etc.) prepared during the project
- DB meetings and site visits
  - Timing and frequency of DB meetings
  - Schedule of regular site visits
  - Representation and attendance at DB meetings and site visits
  - Meeting agendas, summaries of meetings and/or site-visit reports
- Communications
  - Open and transparent sharing of information between the parties and the DB
  - Limitations regarding one-on-one communications between DB members and party representatives
  - Designation of a point of contact for DB communications and transmittal of information and documents

- Dispute avoidance
  - Avoidance of disputes through early identification of potential issues and informal assistance from the DB
  - Dispute avoidance techniques such as advisory opinions, facilitated meetings, etc.
- Dispute resolution
  - Referral of a dispute to the DB
  - Schedule for statements of position by the parties
  - Written submissions and responses by the parties
  - DB hearings
  - DB recommendations and/or decisions
  - Acceptance or rejection of the DB recommendations/decisions

It should be noted that if the formal dispute-resolution process is included in the DB Specification, it does not need to be replicated in the DB Rules/Operating Procedures.

Chapter 9
Dispute Boards in FIDIC Contracts

FIDIC stands for the Fédération International des Ingénieurs-Conseils (International Federation of Consulting Engineers). It is an industry umbrella group based in Geneva, made up of approximately 100 national associations of consulting engineers. The organization was founded in 1913 with the goal of promoting excellence in engineering management, including thorough study and publication of industry best-practice guides.

FIDIC also publishes procurement guides and since 1957 has provided international model forms of construction contracts, which have become world standards. These FIDIC forms of contract are widely used by multilateral development banks (MDBs), government authorities and private parties in many countries. Because of that wide usage, this chapter will capitalize terms in FIDIC documents that FIDIC routinely capitalizes, departing from the style used elsewhere in this manual for most similar references.

For many years, FIDIC has adopted innovative dispute-resolution provisions within its standard form contracts. The synergy between the DRBF and FIDIC dates to the early 1980s with implementation of the first international DB in conjunction with the World Bank-financed El Cajón dam and hydroelectric facility in Honduras. The World Bank at that time was already using FIDIC model forms of contract in its Standard Bidding Documents.

FIDIC currently publishes standard forms adapted to varying contracting methods and types of construction. The best-known forms are known as the Rainbow Suite:

- **The Red Book:** "Conditions of Contract for Construction"
- **The Yellow Book**: "Conditions of Contract for Plant and Design-Build"
- **The Silver Book:** "Conditions of Contract for EPC Turnkey Projects"

Current users of FIDIC forms are likely familiar with the 1999 editions of the Rainbow Suite and the new versions of the Rainbow Suite published in 2017. In cooperation with MDBs, FIDIC published a customized version of The Red Book, with subsequent editions in 2006 and 2010, known as The Pink Book. There is also another form, "Conditions of Contract for Design, Build and Operate Projects," published in 2008 and known as The Gold Book.

Due to inclusion of provisions for DBs in all of FIDIC's standard forms since 1992, together with the endorsement of MDBs, these contracts have become the backbone of international DB usage. Historically, FIDIC used the term "Dispute Adjudication Board" (DAB) to describe the DB process, except in the MDB edition that used the DRBF's preferred term — Dispute Board (DB). The 2017 FIDIC contracts now use the term "Dispute Avoidance/ Adjudication Board" (DAAB).

In 1999, the Rainbow Suite differentiated between design-build contracts (Yellow and Silver books) and contracts where the design was undertaken by the Employer (Red Book). Standing DBs were included in the latter, and ad hoc DBs had been included in the former. However, in the 2017 Rainbow Suite, all three standard forms of contract have adopted standing DBs.

The DRBF recommends the use of standing DBs as opposed to ad hoc types and welcomes this change in the 2017 editions — because it now allows DBs to practice dispute avoidance measures in the design-build and EPC (Engineering, Procurement and Construction) forms as well as the construction form of contract.

The Gold Book features a standing DB during the design-build period, which is replaced by a standing one-person DB for a five-year term, a period renewable by agreement of the parties and the DB member.

The 1999 Rainbow Suite contracts have 20 clauses and follow a standard structure. The clauses address the following subjects:

- Clause 1: general provisions
- Clauses 2-5: the role of the parties, the Engineer and nominated subcontractors

- Clauses 6-7: labor, plant and materials
- Clause 8: time-related matters
- Causes 9-11: completion and defects notification
- Clauses 12-14: financial issues.
- Clauses 15-16: termination provisions
- Clauses 17-19: risks, insurance and force majeure
- Cause 20: claims, disputes and arbitration

In Clause 20, FIDIC adopted a three-tier dispute-resolution mechanism. As the first step, the contract administrator, referred to as the "Engineer," is required to issue a fair determination. Under FIDIC forms of contract, the Engineer's determination must reflect his or her own assessment and determination of the dispute, independently of the Employer's position.

The DB procedure is then the second stage in the mechanism. A FIDIC DB will conduct a procedurally fair process and issue a binding but not final decision on the dispute (see Chapters 14-17). The third stage is arbitration, with the International Chamber of Commerce (ICC) named as the default governing body for the arbitration process.

In the 1999 versions of the FIDIC contract, the DB provisions are set out in Clause 20 (Claim, Dispute and Arbitration).

Key sub-clauses of Clause 20 set out details of the DB process and are described further below. FIDIC standard forms also include a model DB Agreement form with a set of DB Procedural Rules.

Sub-clause 20.2
"Appointment of the Dispute Adjudication Board"

The following provisions govern appointment of the DB pursuant to Sub-clause 20.2.

The DB comprises one or three members depending on which is stipulated in the Appendix to Tender. If the Appendix to Tender is silent, the DB will have three members. For standing DBs under the 1999

Red Book, the DB is to be appointed within 28 days of the Letter of Acceptance being issued to the Contractor by the Employer. Under ad hoc DBs of the Yellow and Silver books, the DB is only appointed after a dispute has arisen.

In accordance with the specified procedure, where it is a three-member DB, each party nominates a DB member for the approval of the other party. A party may reject the other party's nomination at its discretion and without explaining its reasons for the rejection. Once the two co-members of the DB have been agreed to, the parties and the two co-members select the DB Chair through consultation. In the case of a single-member DB, the person is selected by consultation and agreement between the parties.

Sub-Clause 20.2 provides an option to include a list of potential members as an attachment to the contract, which is determined at the bid stage. In the 2017 Rainbow Suite, FIDIC has made the listing of potential DB members in the contract the default procedure rather than simply an option.

Sub-clause 20.3
"Failure to Agree Dispute Adjudication Board"

If the parties are unable to reach agreement on the appointment of DB members, Sub-clause 20.3 sets out a procedure for recourse to an "appointing entity." The appointing entity is to be named in the Appendix to Tender. The most commonly designated institutional entities are the President of FIDIC and the ICC. FIDIC maintains and publishes a list of accredited adjudicators (DB members) who are certified by exam.

The procedure under Sub-clause 20.3 is also applicable if the parties cannot agree on the replacement for a DB member who is unable to act due to death, illness, resignation or termination. In both cases, the appointing entity shall endeavor to consult with both parties, and the subsequent appointment is deemed to be "final and conclusive." FIDIC and the ICC charge a fee for such appointments, which is shared equally by the parties.

Under the 1999 versions of the Rainbow Suite, there are no provisions that enable a party to challenge the position of a sitting DB member. However, in the 2017 editions, FIDIC now permits a party to raise a conflict of interest challenge (see Chapter 5) against a sitting DB member, under a procedure administered by the ICC.

Sub-clause 20.4
"Obtaining Dispute Adjudication Board's Decision"

Despite the best efforts of a DB to avoid disputes, either party may decide to proceed with the formal referral of a dispute to the DB, pursuant to Sub-clause 20.4, for its binding decision.

The DB is then required to set a procedural timetable and render its decision within 84 days of receipt of the referral. An extension to the 84-day period is only possible with the agreement of both parties. Accordingly, the DB should make every effort to expedite the procedure. Under the Procedural Rules of the Red Book, the DB may adopt various procedures, tailored to suit the dispute.

Under the Procedural Rules, the DB is to act fairly and impartially and ensure that due process is respected.

The Dispute Adjudication Agreement

All FIDIC contracts include a model DB Agreement (incorporating a set of General Conditions) and a set of DB Procedural Rules. The principal provisions for DB members and the parties to note are the DB's general obligations under General Condition, Clause 4 and the DB's powers under Procedural Rule 8. Remuneration of the DB is covered under General Condition, Clause 6.

The DB member's obligations under **General Condition, Clause 4** include:

- No financial ties to the parties or the Engineer.
- No previous employment or consulting history with a party except as disclosed before appointment.
- No previous professional or personal relationship with any employee of a party or the Engineer or any previous involvement with the overall project.
- No employment as a consultant or otherwise with any of the parties or the Engineer.
- Complying with the Procedural Rules and Sub-clause 20.4 of the works contract.
- Not giving advice unless requested by both parties.
- Not entering into discussions about future employment with a party or the Engineer.
- Remaining available for site visits and hearings.
- Becoming conversant with the works contract and remaining current with the progress of the works.
- Keeping all DB activities confidential. Any disclosures must have the written consent of both parties and the other DB members.
- Being available to give advice and opinions when requested by both parties.

The DB's powers under **Procedural Rule 8** include:

- Establishing the procedure for deciding a dispute.
- Deciding upon the DB's own jurisdiction and the scope of the dispute.
- Conducting hearings as the DB deems fit, in accordance with the Procedural Rules.
- Taking the initiative in ascertaining the facts required for a decision.
- Making use of the DB's own specialist knowledge.
- Deciding upon the payment of financing charges.
- Deciding upon any interim or conservatory measures.
- Opening up, reviewing and revising any certificate, decision, determination, instruction, opinion or valuation of the Engineer.

General Condition, Clause 6 stipulates the terms of the DB members' remuneration, including provisions for a retainer and daily fees (see Chapter 11).

The retainer fee covers maintaining availability on 28 days' notice for all site visits and hearings, read-in time between site visits and all office and overhead expenses of the DB member.

The daily fee covers all time spent on site visits, including up to two days' travel in each direction and all time spent in connection with a formal referral of a dispute for a DB decision, or a request for the DB's advice or an opinion.

Travel expenses are reimbursed at cost; although, air fares and the retainer are to be paid quarterly in advance. Importantly, taxes levied on the DB member's services in the country where the project is located are the responsibility of the parties, provided the DB member is not a fiscal resident of that country.

Payment to DB members is generally made by the Contractor, who in turn includes a request for reimbursement from the Employer for one-half of the payment in its monthly statements. The Contractor and the Employer are jointly and severally liable for payment of DB invoices.

Some important changes to the above provisions were made in the 2017 editions of the Rainbow Suite, including:

- DB members are to invoice each party 50% of their retainer and daily fee; although, there is an option for the Contractor to remain the paymaster (as in the 1999 editions).
- The DB Agreement is deemed to be signed in cases where the DB is appointed by a nominating authority and one of the parties is not cooperative.
- The applicable law of the DB Agreement is stipulated to be the same as the law of the Contract.

Site Visits

According to Procedural Rule 1, a standing DB should schedule site visits every 70 to 140 days, depending on the stage of construction.

Most projects using FIDIC forms of contract will have at least one international DB member, and site visits will typically take place over two to four days in the country where the project is located. Due to distances involved, it is common to schedule hearings of disputed matters at the same time as the regular DB site visit and meeting, to economize on travel costs.

For DBs in remote locations, international DB members will typically arrive in a major city near the project on the day before the site visit and transfer to the project site on day one of the visit. A typical agenda will include brief presentations of progress by the Engineer and a physical tour of the site. Any remaining time on day one and day two will be allocated to discussions of matters of concern, with the parties and the Engineer answering the DB's questions.

In their dispute avoidance role (see Chapter 13), DB members should encourage the parties to take immediate action on matters that are harming, or may harm, the project's schedule or that carry a risk of increasing costs. The DB may also offer to provide opinions on any matter it deems appropriate.

Under the Procedural Rules for standing DBs, the DB is required to prepare a site-visit report before leaving the site. It is common to allow day three of a visit for the preparation and discussion of the site-visit report before the DB members depart.

Because the DB, the parties and the Engineer may all have to travel for several hours to the site and may be lodging in the same hotels, DB members must pay particular attention to the logistical arrangements, to avoid any DB member being in a compromising situation where they have to travel or spend time with one party only (see Chapter 6).

The Dispute Resolution Procedure

The content of a referral to the DB may vary from little more than a basic statement of the dispute, which requires further development within 84 days, to a lengthy and detailed statement of the case. Many standing DBs will brief the parties at the outset of its appointment as to which form of presentation of the dispute the DB prefers.

A typical procedure will call for a position paper from the opposing (respondent) party in its defense within approximately 28 to 35 days. But if the initial referral was submitted in summary format, it is usually necessary to instruct the claimant party to submit a complete position paper as the first step of the procedure.

The position papers should explain the factual nature of the dispute and the respective contractual and legal arguments in support of the claim and the defense. The papers (see Chapter 15) should be accompanied by supporting documentation of facts relied upon and a schedule analysis if matters of delay are concerned. The position papers should also set out the parties' positions on valuation of the dispute.

Within a short time after receipt of the referral, the DB should seek the parties' views on whether they wish a hearing. If they do, this step must be integrated into the procedural calendar, and the procedure for the hearing should also be discussed (see Chapter 16). It is recommended that a hearing, if any, take place no later than day 60 from the start of the 84-day contractual time limit to render a decision, in order to allow the DB sufficient time to deliberate and prepare the decision following the hearing.

Under the Procedural Rules, the DB may conduct the hearing as it sees fit and can adopt an inquisitorial procedure, a common procedure in civil law countries. The DB may deny participation in the hearing of any persons other than the parties and the Engineer (see Chapter 16). If necessary the DB may proceed ex parte (with only one party present), provided the absent party has been informed of the date, time and location of the hearing and has been afforded all reasonable opportunity to attend. Under the Procedural Rules, the DB is not to express any opinions on the merits of the case during the hearings.

The DB's decision must be reasoned, and, pursuant to Sub-clause 20.6, will be admissible in arbitration, though DB members cannot be called as witnesses. The DB decision is immediately binding on the parties and must be given effect unless, and until, it is replaced, either by an amicable settlement between the parties or by a subsequent arbitral award.

Should either party disagree with the DB decision, it is important for that party to issue a notice of dissatisfaction to the other party within 28 days to preserve the disagreeing party's right to begin arbitration at a later date. Failure to issue such a notice will usually result in the DB decision becoming final and binding and the loss of the dissatisfied party's right to arbitrate.

If a notice of dissatisfaction has been issued, the FIDIC contract provisions do not set out a time limit for starting arbitration; however, the statute of limitations under applicable law will apply.

If a party does not comply with the DB's decision, the other party may begin arbitration proceedings. The claimant then commonly requests the arbitral tribunal to first issue a Partial Award obliging the defaulting party to comply with the DB decision, as a preliminary matter before the tribunal considers the merits of the defaulting party's case.

For various reasons, arbitral tribunals will sometimes decline a request to issue such "pay now, argue later" orders. Legal advice is essential before starting arbitration so that the dissatisfied party is aware of the risks of proceeding beyond the DB.

2017 Editions of the Rainbow Suite

The 2017 editions of the Rainbow Suite include the following clarifications and additions to FIDIC's earlier DB dispute resolution process:

- If the DB has concerns over delays or default on payment for its services, it may withhold the publication of the decision pending payment of its fees and expenses. This was previously only permitted in the 1999 editions of the Yellow and Silver books.
- The 2017 editions clarify that a party may give a partial notice of dissatisfaction. In such a case, the part of the decision that is not the subject of the notice shall become final and binding.
- A new Sub-clause 21.7 (Failure to Comply with DAAB's Decision) has clarified the arbitral tribunal's power to order a defaulting party to comply with a DB decision before proceeding on the merits. However, mandatory applicable law in some jurisdictions may constrain this power.
- Under new Procedural Rule 8, the DB may now correct mathematical and typographical errors (under certain conditions) following publication of the DB's decision.

Advisory Opinions

In addition to using regular DB meetings and site visits to stimulate discussion about how to resolve issues and claims before they become formal disputes, the DB may issue written Advisory Opinions and give advice under specific circumstances and conditions.

In many countries, the parties find it useful to take advantage of this power of the DB to give nonbinding advice and opinions. Both parties are required, however, to make a request in writing to the DB before it is permitted to proceed with this option. Use of the Advisory Opinion is also recommended by the DRBF as an effective dispute-avoidance mechanism (see Chapter 13). The DB's authority to issue opinions and give advice can be found in the following provisions of the 1999 edition of the FIDIC Red Book:

- *Sub-clause 20.2 (Appointment of the Dispute Adjudication Board):* If the parties both agree, they may jointly refer a matter to the DB for its opinion.
- *Clause 4(k) of the DB Agreement:* A DB member is to be available to give advice and opinions on any matter when requested by both parties.

- *Clause 2 of the DB Agreement (Pink Book only):* The DB should endeavor to prevent potential problems or claims from becoming disputes.

While not changing the DB's actual role, the 2017 editions of the Rainbow Suite have clarified and emphasized the importance of these dispute-avoidance techniques. Sub-clause 21.3 (Avoidance of Disputes) and Procedural Rule 2 provide an expanded description of dispute avoidance powers attributed to the DB.

In many countries, the use of Advisory Opinions has proven to be effective. When dispute avoidance is promoted by the DB and widely practiced, resolution rates are high and significant time and cost benefits flow to the project.

DB members report that the relative success of the Advisory Opinion process may be due to the fact the parties have both agreed to submit the matter to the DB for advice or an opinion, which indicates a mutual desire to resolve the dispute amicably. There is also the "back-stop" effect, given that the DB retains its authority to issue a decision if the dispute continues and a party deems it necessary to submit a formal referral.

While the DB is entitled to change its opinion if it has to issue a binding decision, many parties rightly view a DB's opinion as an opportunity to assess the weakness and strength of their respective positions and the likelihood of success if the matter were to be pursued to the next level.

Termination of the Dispute Board

There are several ways for the DB's mandate to expire or to terminate the DB under FIDIC forms of contract:

- The DB may be terminated by both parties upon 42 days' notice. However, a single party acting alone may not terminate the DB member it appointed, or the DB as whole.
- The DB may also be terminated by the issuance of a "discharge" signed by the Contractor after agreement of the

Final Statement, which occurs after the end of the Defects Notification Period (Sub-clause 14.12).

- A DB member may resign by giving 70 days' notice. This time period has been reduced to 28 days in the 2017 Rainbow Suite editions, under General Condition 10.1 of the DB Agreement.
- Under the 1999 Yellow and Silver books, the ad hoc DB's mandate expires after issue of the DB decision, unless a further referral is filed before the last decision is issued. This has caused difficulties in cases where a party wishes to submit a further referral after the ad hoc DB's mandate has expired, as it is not uncommon for at least one of the parties to refuse to reappoint the original DB. Therefore, due to this issue, the parties may amend the DB expiration provisions in the dispute-adjudication agreement to allow the DB to be placed on standby between decisions. Such amendments usually include further clarification that the DB members will not be entitled to a retainer fee and that the expiration of the DB's mandate is tied to the issuance of the discharge.

Chapter 10
Dispute Boards in Public-Private Partnership Contracts

A Public-Private Partnership (PPP) is a government-owned, public project where development, construction and/or operation of the project is funded by private financing (equity or debt or both). In some countries, the acronym PPP is reduced to "P3."

PPPs are an increasingly popular form of procurement for infrastructure and major development projects across the world. These projects are typically undertaken to produce public infrastructure in such industry sectors as transport, energy and water. PPP projects include roads, bridges, tunnels, railways, water operations, ports and airports.

In some countries, PPPs also involve what are called "social PPP projects" to develop accommodation-based facilities in housing, education, sport, health and prisons. The benefits of PPPs are that they deliver for the public sector projects that may otherwise be unaffordable, that are seen as "value for money" for both government and the public at large.

PPPs can take different forms and can be seen at various stages of evolution in many countries. As far as form is concerned, there are two main types — the availability-based arrangement, where the public authority pays the private provider a fee for the asset or service; and the concession arrangement, where the provider of the public asset or service is paid by the user. These arrangements are described in more detail below.

In short, a PPP can be described as a partnership through a contracted arrangement (also known as a concession contract) between a public authority or government and a private partner for provision of an asset — which the private partner finances, designs, builds or rehabilitates, operates and maintains, and from which services are delivered to the public.

Based on the type of PPP (see below), the asset is paid for by the public authority through a fee over the lifetime of the contract (availability-based payment structure), from users' fees (concession-based payment structure) or a combination of both. The fundamental feature of a PPP project is the provision of hard or social infrastructure and/or services by a private entity to, or on behalf of, a public entity.

Common Features of a PPP

The common features of both an availability-based PPP and a concession-based PPP are:

- The private sector party contracting with the public sector will normally be a limited liability company set up specifically for the project by its funders/shareholders and referred to as the Special Purpose Vehicle (SPV). It is often referred to as the "project company," "ProjectCo" or "ServiceCo."
- The SPV is required to design, construct or rehabilitate, operate and maintain an asset or item of infrastructure that provides a service to the public sector. At times, this may involve taking over an existing asset.
- The SPV will use private financing to fund upfront development and construction costs. The usual split is around 80-20 or 90-10 in favor of private debt, with the smaller percentage coming from private equity, usually SPV shareholders. In less developed countries, this funding may come from Multilateral Development Banks, known as "MDBs," or other international funding and development agencies such as the World Bank.
- The SPV will enter into a contract or a series of contracts (which are, in effect, sub-contracts) with the design-build (D&B) contractor and the operator and maintainer (O&M) of the asset. These contracts transfer most of the risks, which the SPV has assumed from the public authority (via the concession contract), to the relevant contractor. This pass-through or sub-contracting of the risks will normally be insisted upon by lenders to the project.

- Forms of procurement for PPP projects are more complex than conventional public procurement because of the public services being delivered and the hierarchy of contracts used.
- The contract period (or concession period) is often 15 to 30 years or more. Lenders, because of the size and long-term nature of their investment, have a strong influence on how risk is allocated down the contract chain.
- There are obvious friction points or risk interfaces within these projects, and they constitute a fundamental reason for the existence and success of DBs within the PPP project structure.

Availability-Based PPP

The diagram below indicates an availability-based PPP structure.

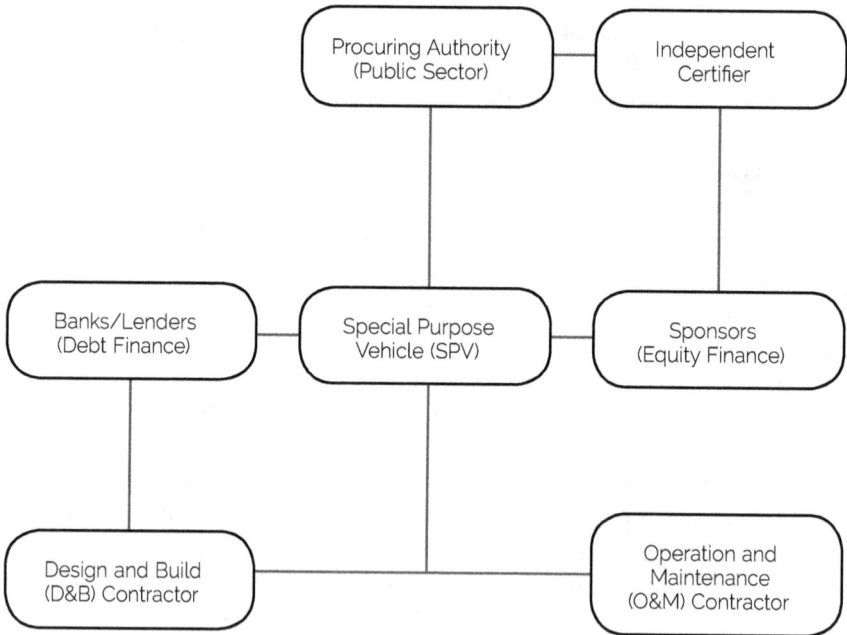

```
┌────────────────────┐          ┌──────────────────┐
│ Procuring Authority │─────────│   Independent     │
│   (Public Sector)   │          │    Certifier      │
└────────────────────┘          └──────────────────┘
          │                              │
          │                              │
┌──────────────┐   ┌─────────────────┐  ┌──────────────┐
│ Banks/Lenders │──│ Special Purpose  │──│   Sponsors    │
│ (Debt Finance)│   │  Vehicle (SPV)   │  │(Equity Finance)│
└──────────────┘   └─────────────────┘  └──────────────┘
       │                                        │
┌──────────────┐                    ┌──────────────────┐
│Design and Build│                   │  Operation and    │
│(D&B) Contractor│───────────────────│   Maintenance     │
└──────────────┘                    │ (O&M) Contractor  │
                                     └──────────────────┘
```

The availability-based PPP has the following distinguishing features:

- The SPV is paid a periodic fee by the procuring authority from the point at which the contracted asset is available for use. This is often called the availability fee and will include principal and interest payments on the debt, a return to the private sector sponsors and an amount for the services delivered.
- The SPV's only income is the availability fee. This fee is paid according to the extent that the asset is available for use or services provided in accordance with contractually agreed upon service levels.

Concession PPP

The diagram below indicates a concession-based PPP structure.

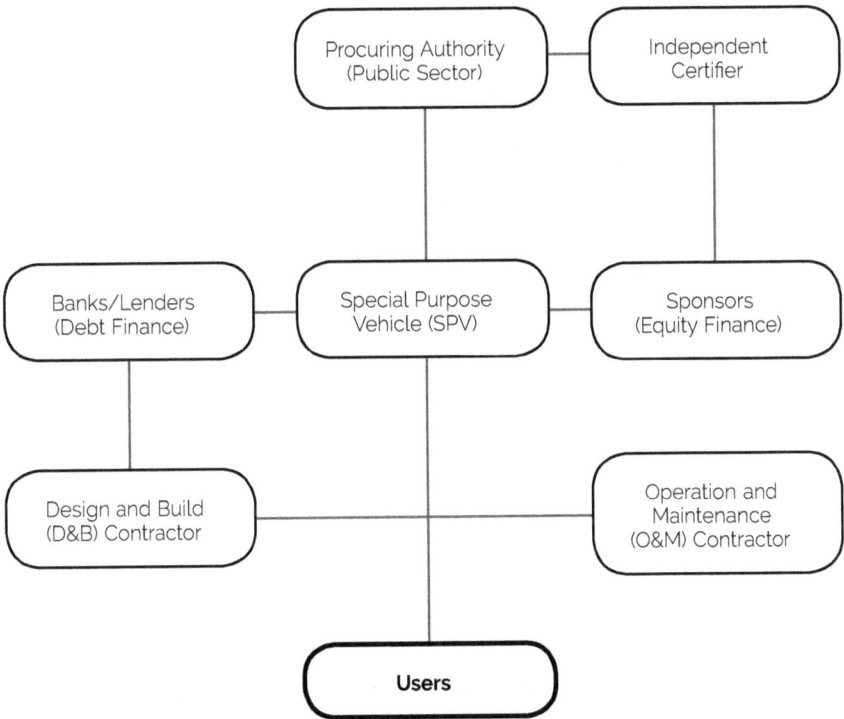

In concession PPPs, the SPV is delegated the full operation of the public facility, such as a highway, bridge, rail system or stadium, to name a few common examples. This usually involves the design, construction or rehabilitation, operation and maintenance of the asset or infrastructure.

The distinguishing features are:

- The SPV is in a direct relationship with the end users of the services. In turn, the SPV receives fees from these users to recover its investment entirely (or almost entirely). Examples of such fees are road tolls, entry fees, usage charges, etc.
- The SPV, therefore, takes the risk of the sufficiency of such fees to provide an appropriate return on its investment.
- The SPV also takes the risk over the lifetime of the project that it can meet and adapt to the changing demands/needs of the end user, in a way that the availability-based PPP does not.

Dispute Avoidance and Resolution in PPPs

In a PPP project, the potential for disputes among contracting parties is high. Plus, the imperative to avoid such disputes and maintain working relationships over the lifetime of the PPP project is even greater than in a typical contract situation. That's because PPP projects often provide essential public services and because of the long duration of the contracts.

In some countries, PPP contracts are well developed, standardized and have mandatory forms of contracts. The contracts can be extremely complex and detailed. There is little or no opportunity for contractors to negotiate the key terms and risk allocations, or the terms that cover dispute avoidance and dispute resolution.

Furthermore, the practice in the availability-based PPP is to provide for the same dispute-resolution process in each contract within the structure, with some minor differences, to minimize contradictory decisions on the same issues. This requires detailed provisions to address interface risks and to bind the D&B contractor and the O&M contractor to the overall dispute-resolution process within the PPP agreement. These are some of the challenges faced with the inclusion of DBs within the PPP structures.

The DRBF has observed DBs successfully operating in PPPs in several countries. Some of these DBs are, in fact, panels of individuals — technical, financial and legal — who can be called upon to deal with disputes when they arise. Because of their temporary nature and restricted scope to the dispute in question, these DBs do not perform any dispute-avoidance functions. The situation is different in Australia, where there are examples of DBs, established as standing boards, being extremely successful in assisting the PPP parties to avoid potentially project-threatening disputes.

One question that arises is the cost of a standing DB over the lifetime of a PPP project and the perception that the expense cannot be justified, at least during the operational phase. This is often why DBs are limited to the construction phase and a short time after commissioning. Putting figures on the benefits and savings that may be achieved by the presence of a standing DB (see Chapter 2) is a research task currently being pursued by the DRBF.

Options for Dispute Boards in PPP Projects

There are various models for DBs on a PPP project, in both availability and concession PPPs. These models include:

1. One DB covering both the concession and the D&B contract.
2. Three separate DBs, with one covering the concession contract, one covering the D&B contract and one covering the early years of the O&M contract.
3. Separate DBs for the concession contract, and one covering the D&B contract and the early years of the O&M contract.
4. One DB at the concession-contract level only, with a standing invitation for the D&B contractor to attend the concession DB meetings.
5. One DB at the D&B contract level only (where most of the risks are transferred).

There is no one best model for DBs on a PPP project, and the best model depends on the risk appetite and experience of the primary participants — the procuring authority, the D&B contractor and the lenders.

The DRBF recommends choosing Options 1 to 4 above, depending upon the nature of the PPP. Option 5 is not recommended.

Requirements for Successful Dispute Boards in PPP Projects

The DRBF recommends the following principles for DBs within PPP projects:

- DB(s) should be established at the beginning of the PPP project and operate for at least the duration of any construction period and the initial operation and maintenance period.
- Given the multilayered nature of PPP projects and the many stakeholders, the DRBF recommends a DB be included as part of the dispute-avoidance regime (see Chapter 13) in the two major contracts (concession and D&B), if not all contracts, within the PPP structure.
- For PPP contracts with lengthy operational phases (particularly availability-based models), it is useful for the tenure of the DB to extend into the operational phase or, alternatively, a different DB can be appointed for the operational phase. The duration of the DB's term may vary depending upon the nature of the project and the stakeholders.
- The key to success for a DB within a PPP project is that the DB consists of appropriately experienced members (see Chapter 5). It is essential that DB members have an understanding of the financial and commercial aspects of PPPs.
- Skills and expertise required of DB members may also change over the lifetime of the DB. It is recommended that provision be made for replacement or additional DB members when the project enters the operational phase.

- If there is only one DB at the concession level, the main delivery sub-contractors should be bound into the operation and decisions of the DB established at that level. Without this arrangement, there is likely to be a fragmentation of approach and inconsistent and conflicting decision-making.

Chapter 11

Costs and Fees

Fee structures and costs of the DB process vary considerably worldwide. Information in this chapter is based on the DRBF's historical records covering several thousand DBs and from surveys of DRBF members. Examples of typical DB costs are noted for projects in the U.S., Australasia, Latin America and other countries that use the FIDIC contract forms of DB. For convenience and comparison purposes, all costs noted in this chapter are expressed in U.S. dollars, at 2019 rates.

Dispute Board Cost Components

Factors that typically determine the costs of a DB over the life of a project are:

- Size of the DB (for example, three persons or one person).
- Frequency and duration of DB meetings.
- Number of formal referrals to the DB
  for opinions/recommendations/decisions.
- Type and level of fees (for example, hourly, daily and for travel) paid to DB members.
- Reimbursable expenses for DB members, including subsistence and travel to remote sites, interstate or internationally.
- Retainers paid to DB members.
- Fee adjustments over the duration of the project.

The frequency of regular DB meetings often differs from project to project, based on the nature of the work, the requirements of the parties and the stage the project has reached. DBs for heavy civil and underground construction projects usually meet quarterly (more frequently in the initial stages of the project), while DBs on vertical/building projects often meet monthly. DBs on other types of projects with a very long duration (more than five years) may only meet every four to six months. For all projects, if DB hearings are required to deal with the parties' referral of disputes to the DB, the actual number of DB meetings will be correspondingly greater.

Fee levels for DB members will usually reflect typical rates paid for similar professional services in the local region but may vary depending upon the country and the nature of the project. Moreover, in situations where DB members are not based locally, the fees for those DB members are likely to correspond to the usual rates paid for DB services in their home country.

Reimbursable expenses are dependent on the location of the project and the proximity to each DB member's home base. When DB members live in close proximity to the project, travel costs will be minimal. When projects are remote, or when DB members must travel significant distances to the project site, they will incur expenses for meals, lodging, ground transport and possibly air travel. In these situations, the reimbursable expenses will become a relevant factor in determining the total cost of the DB process.

A retainer is the generic name for a lump-sum fee paid to a DB member to retain his or her services. When used, retainers are generally paid on a monthly basis to compensate DB members for work outside of DB meetings, such as reviewing project documents (minutes of site meetings, reports and other correspondence), keeping abreast of project developments and carrying out DB administrative activities. Retainers are also intended to act as compensation for DB members who must remain available to serve on the DB throughout its duration, thereby foregoing other professional work opportunities.

Types of Dispute Board Fee Structures

Owners will generally include a proposed DB fee structure within the DB Agreement; although, in some cases, it may be possible for potential DB members to negotiate their own preferred fee arrangements before entering into the DB Agreement. DB fee structures will generally include some or all of the following components.

Daily Rate

DB members will usually be paid a fixed daily rate for their services. The daily rate is intended to compensate DB members for their services in attending meetings and hearings and, in some cases, for local travel and work carried out between meetings. However, when a full day's work or travel is not involved, an hourly rate is often utilized.

Hourly Rate

In this case, DB members are paid a fixed hourly rate. The hourly rate may be the basis of payment for all DB activities or, alternatively, only for tasks undertaken between regular DB meetings, such as reviewing documents, writing reports, etc.

Retainer

DB fee structures may include a retainer to ensure the availability of DB members and, in many cases, to compensate them (in lieu of an hourly rate) for time spent in reviewing project documents and other activities between DB meetings. A retainer is paid as a fixed monthly rate and is sometimes referred to as a "monthly management fee."

Travel Time

Where travel time is significant, DB fee structures usually include a fee or allowance, either separately or as a percentage of the hourly or daily rate, for time spent by DB members when traveling between their home base and the location of the project. For most DBs, the actual costs of travel (airfares, ground transport, etc.) are paid as a reimbursable expense. Local travel costs are generally not reimbursable.

Reimbursable Expenses

Expenses incurred by a DB member in performing his or her DB role, including meals, airfares, accommodation and ground transport, are usually reimbursed at cost, based on evidence of payment. Some governmental agencies and institutional DB rules have restrictions that limit the type or amount of reimbursable expenses that can be claimed (for example, class of air travel or a cap on total daily expenses).

Fee Adjustments

For projects lasting more than two years, some DB fee structures include an annual escalation of fee levels. The percentage adjustment of the DB fee rates will depend upon the annual rate of inflation and the relative value of the currency in the country where the project is located.

Typical Fee Structures and Rates

Typical fee structures and fee rates for DBs in different parts of the world are illustrated in the following examples. As noted earlier, all fee levels listed below are expressed in U.S. dollars at 2019 prices. These examples are not intended to be used for any purpose other than as a general guide and comparison of DB costs and DB members' fees.

United States

Fee arrangements for DB members in the U.S. differ considerably between states and with different owners. Where hourly rates are used, they generally range from $125 to $300 per hour. If daily rates are used, they generally range from $1,200 to $2,500 per day.

Reimbursement for travel expenses ranges from nothing (considered to be part of the daily rate) to actual expenses, based on approved governmental and other travel guidelines.

For some major projects, fee rates are negotiated between the DB members and the parties. However, the ranges noted above for hourly and daily rates are much more common. The three examples that follow indicate the wide variability of fee structures and rates for DB members in the U.S.

1. The California Department of Transportation (Caltrans) pays each DB member a lump-sum daily rate of $1,500 for each regular DB meeting or hearing day and compensates members at the rate of $150 per hour for document reviews and DB activities between

meetings. No mileage, travel, lodging or per diem expenses are reimbursed. The daily rate of $1,500 is intended to compensate for travel costs and participation in the DB meeting or hearing. These lump-sum fee rates are set within the Caltrans DB Specification and do not usually vary among DB members or between projects.

2. The Colorado Department of Transportation (CDOT) pays each DB member a lump sum of $800 for DB meetings of one to four hours and $1,200 for meetings of four to eight hours. CDOT compensates DB members at the rate of $125 per hour for document reviews and DB activities between meetings. DB members receive $50 per hour for travel expenses, and no other reimbursement is provided. These rates are established in the CDOT DB Specification and do not vary among DB members or projects.

3. The Washington State Department of Transportation (WSDOT) pays each DB member an hourly rate for all time spent in meetings, hearings, travel to and from meetings and in DB activities and reviews between meetings. Hourly rates are negotiated with each DB member individually and range from $175 to $275 per hour. WSDOT also reimburses DB members for travel costs and pays a per diem allowance up to a maximum amount allowed in WSDOT travel regulations. At the time of publication, WSDOT has indicated it would also be implementing a daily rate structure in the near future.

Australia, New Zealand, Pacific Islands

Fee arrangements for DB members in Australia, New Zealand and the Pacific Islands will vary based on location, project size and the DB member's experience. The DB Chair, usually more experienced and with a greater workload, is likely to receive a higher fee than the other DB members. DB members usually negotiate their fees as part of their offer of DB services to the parties. Occasionally, some owners will specify standard fee rates within the DB Agreement.

Hourly rates range from about US$300 to US$450 per person for a three-person DB. Daily rates will generally be based on a multiple of seven or eight hours at the hourly rate. Fees for one-person DBs in Australia are similar but are usually at the high end of the range noted above for three-person DBs, in recognition of the greater workload.

Fee structures are different in the Pacific Islands. Projects are typically funded by development agencies, which use FIDIC forms of contract. Hourly rates range from US$150 to US$250, and DB appointments may depend on a competitive selection process that includes the DB nominee's proposed fee levels.

Retainers (if applicable) will generally be structured on a monthly basis and set at about half the daily fee rate. Travel costs are usually reimbursed separately on an actual cost basis, with supporting receipts as evidence of payment.

Latin America
Fee arrangements for DB members in Latin America generally follow the structure used in FIDIC contracts (see below). A daily fee is paid for attendance at DB meetings, hearings, site visits and for drafting DB recommendations or decisions. A monthly retainer is also paid in most countries to cover all other DB work.

Current fee levels vary depending upon the country and the characteristics of the specific project. Daily fee rates for DB members range from US$1,250 to US$1,800. Monthly retainers range from US$2,500 to US$4,000.

Fee rates may also vary depending on a DB member's experience, qualifications and whether he or she is a local resident of the country where the project is located.

FIDIC Contracts
DB fee structures within FIDIC contracts are generally based on a daily rate for attendance at DB meetings and hearings, travel time and time spent on DB deliberations and drafting of DB decisions. Travel and subsistence expenses are reimbursed separately. Monthly retainers are often utilized.

Daily fees are paid after they have been incurred or at a relevant time within the DB process, such as at the delivery of a DB decision/opinion. Retainers (when applicable) are usually invoiced quarterly in advance. The 1999 FIDIC Plant and Design Build and EPC Turnkey contract editions, as well as all the 2017 editions of the FIDIC contracts, allow for the DB to withhold publication of a decision pending full payment of DB fees.

Current fee levels for three-person FIDIC DBs vary widely. Daily rates for DB members generally range from US$2,000 to US$5,000, depending on a DB member's experience, qualifications and country of residence. In some countries, daily rates for local DB members may be below US$2,000. It is not uncommon to include an hourly rate in the fee schedule, based on dividing the daily rate by seven or eight (hours) to cover partial days worked by DB members on dispute-avoidance activities and referrals.

The DB Chair will usually earn a higher base fee level to reflect his/her professional qualifications and experience. There is generally no premium added for the key role but the DB Chair will usually earn more due to additional time spent on management and administrative tasks.

FIDIC fee levels are fixed for the first 24 months of the DB's term and are then adjusted annually. However, there is no provision for fee escalation in the 2017 editions of FIDIC contracts. The fees are usually agreed to be net of taxes in the country of the project, including for DB members not resident in that country.

Retainers, where applicable, will generally be structured on a monthly basis. It is common practice that monthly retainers are equal to the daily fee. On occasion, the parties may request that DB members forego their retainer. However, this means DB members will not have been paid for read-in time prior to site visits, reducing the efficacy of the DB's dispute-avoidance activities and the utility of DB visits to the project.

Travel costs are reimbursed separately on an actual cost basis, with supporting receipts as evidence of payment. Travel time (up to a maximum of two days in each direction) is charged at the daily fee. Air travel is stipulated as not less than business class. Expenses are paid after they are incurred — with the notable exception of standing DBs under the 1999 Construction edition and the 2017 editions of FIDIC contracts, where expenses and retainers are billed quarterly in advance and credited/debited according to actual costs incurred.

IFI Financed Contracts

Multilateral Development Banks (MDBs) such as the World Bank have donors from many countries as opposed to Unilateral Development Banks that have a single nation donor. Together, they are referred to as International Financing Institutions (IFIs).

Projects being funded by IFIs will often have a mandatory requirement for a DB. Projects being funded by IFIs will often have a mandatory requirement for a DB. The DRBF recommends IFIs fund 100% of costs where it is mandatory. In practice, some cover only 50%, or none at all, in the funding package. DBs are commonly found on IFI-funded projects when FIDIC Conditions of Contract are used. Fee arrangements for these DBs are therefore the same as for FIDIC DBs and include a daily fee for attendance at DB meetings, hearings and site visits. A monthly retainer is paid during the construction phase of the project, reducing to half or two-thirds of the rate during the Defects Notification Period, depending on which form of FIDIC contract is used.

General Method for Estimating the Cost of a Dispute Board

As previously noted, the cost of a DB will depend upon the duration of the project, the number of DB members, the frequency and duration of DB meetings and hearings, the DB members' travel expenses and the DB fee structure itself.

As an example, for a project with a three-person DB that meets quarterly and has a project duration of two years, the direct and overhead costs of the DB can be simply estimated as follows.

- ***Direct costs*** = [3 members x 4 meetings per year x 2 years duration x the daily fee per member] + [3 members x 24 months x the monthly retainer (if applicable) per member].
- ***Overhead costs*** = the estimated travel expenses (including fares, accommodations, etc.) incurred by each DB member in 8 trips to visit the project site and attend meetings.

For a project where the DB is actively engaged in dispute avoidance and no disputes ultimately emerge, there is likely to be no need for hearings outside the scheduled quarterly DB meetings. However, a **contingency allowance** (say, 20%) should always be included in the project budget for the cost of additional hearings and the associated costs of the DB in dealing with the referral and resolution of disputes.

Two examples of calculating a project budget estimate for a DB are set out below, one a typical DB and the second a multi-national project utilizing a FIDIC form of contract.

Example 1

The cost of a DB on a project valued at $250 million, with a duration of 24 months and quarterly DB meetings, assuming a daily fee rate of $2000 per member, a monthly retainer of $2000 per member and travel to/from the project in a single day, is estimated as follows:

Direct costs = [3 members x 4 meetings x 2 years x $2000/day] + [$2000/monthly retainer x 3 members x 24 months] = $192,000

If the maximum allowed by the owner's travel policy is $750/day/member, an estimate of travel expenses for the DB is:

Overhead costs = 3 members x 8 trips x $750 = $18,000

Contingency allowance for referrals = 20% x $210,000 = $42,000

Thus, the Total Budget Cost of DB = $252,000 (0.1% of the project cost).

Example 2

Using the Japan International Cooperation Agency's guidance note for calculating a budget estimate for DB fees and expenses, the cost of a DB on an "international" project valued at $600 million with a duration of three years, assuming a two-day site visit on a quarterly basis, a daily fee rate of $3,000 per member, a monthly retainer of $3,000 per member and travel to/from the project requiring three days, is estimated as follows:

Retainers = [$3,000/monthly retainer during construction x 3 members x 36 months] + [$1,500/monthly retainer during DNP x 3 members x 12 months] = $378,000

Site Visits and Travel = [$3,000 x 3 members x 6 days x 4 visits x 3 years] + [3 members x 12 meetings x $5,000 (estimated travel expenses)] = $828,000

Contingency Allowance for referrals (with hearings) = 20% x $1,206,000 = $241,200

Thus, the Total Budget Cost of DB = $1,447,200 (0.24% of the project cost)

Payment Arrangements

Administrative arrangements for the payment of fees and expenses to DB members are usually specified in the DB Agreement.

In some cases, the contractor will pay all three DB members from a pay item within the contract schedules, while occasionally, payment may be made solely by the owner/employer. In some international contracts, the contractor is obliged to pay the DB's fee invoices and then back-charge 50% to the owner.

In the majority of DBs, however, each party shares the payment of DB fees equally. With this arrangement, each DB member submits an invoice to each party for 50% of the total amount due to that member.

In some instances, the DB Agreement will include details as to how the relevant financial arrangements are to be implemented. Details relating to the parties' accounting procedures, such as registering as a vendor in the parties' accounts payable systems, should be ascertained before the DB commences work. Payment terms, including time limits for payment after the submission of invoices, are usually specified. If not, the DB Chair should ensure that appropriate arrangements are agreed to with the parties.

FIDIC Contracts

FIDIC contracts generally have more complex payment arrangements. Under the 1999 FIDIC editions and the MDB Edition (2010), DB members invoice the contractor for their fees, who in turn includes 50% of the DB's cost in its monthly payment claim to the owner. Under the 2017 FIDIC editions, DB members invoice each party for 50% of their fees, including retainer and expenses, unless otherwise agreed.

Ad hoc DB members appointed under FIDIC Plant and Design Build and the EPC Turnkey editions (1999) may invoice a 25% advance on estimated fees, plus provide an estimate of total expenses, immediately after the DB Agreement takes effect. Payment is due from the contractor upon receipt of the invoice, and DB members are not obliged to begin their work until payment has been received.

Tax and currency issues, which are relevant in some international locations, should be addressed in advance. The DB Agreement should state whether local taxes or deductions are included in the DB fee rates and/or are reimbursable. For some countries, DB members may be well-advised to consult a professional tax adviser. The DB Agreement should also be clear about the currency to be used for payment. Due to currency fluctuations, DB members should consider including the applicable exchange rate on their invoices at the time of invoicing.

Costs of DB-Appointed Experts

Occasionally, with the parties' approval, DBs may appoint local legal advisers or technical experts to provide specialist advice during a referral. Although this is not a routine practice, parties should be made aware of and agree to this potential expense, which is normally reimbursed at cost.

4

Dispute Boards – Implementation and Process

Chapter 12

Nomination and Appointment of Dispute Board Members

This chapter contains important information that contracting parties should consider when nominating or approving candidates for appointment as DB members. The importance of DB member selection to the overall success of the DB process cannot be overemphasized. The chapter also outlines commonly used appointment processes and procedures.

Candidate Requirements

An essential element of the DB process is that both parties accept, and are satisfied with, all DB members. For both parties to be confident that DB nominees are impartial and independent, the nominees must not have any actual or perceived conflicts of interest. If either party is concerned about a nominee's impartiality and independence, it should exercise its right to reject that candidate. If this step is not taken prior to appointment, the entire DB process will be compromised and is likely to be ineffective.

To enable both parties to be fully informed, those seeking to be nominated as a DB member should provide the parties with a detailed curriculum vitae and a disclosure statement that includes a declaration of associations and interests. The disclosure statement should identify any known or potential conflicts of interest, or circumstances that could be perceived as a conflict of interest (see Chapters 5 and 6).

In instances where a conflict of interest clearly exists, the DB nominee should decline the nomination on his or her own initiative. However, if the declared conflict is remote, or if the declaration has been made to ensure full transparency, it is recommended that the DB nominee include a statement that he or she considers him/herself to be impartial and independent and thus capable of serving on the DB, despite the declaration. The parties then have the option of agreeing to accept the nominee, based on the knowledge of his or her declaration. A good general rule for DB nominees is: if in doubt, always disclose.

Disclosure Statements

To enable DB nominees to provide a complete disclosure statement, they need to be informed as to the names of the parties to the proposed contract, the names of key stakeholders in the project and, where possible, the names of consultants and key senior management of both the owner and the contractor. DB nominees should also be provided with details of the project and the terms of the proposed DB Agreement that they will be required to enter into with the parties.

It is recommended that a typical disclosure statement should contain:

- An acknowledgement of the entities or persons involved in the project (as supplied by the parties, or by reference to an attached list).
- A declaration of all relationships and interests that are actual or potential conflicts of interest.
- A general declaration of the DB nominee's professional activities in the industry.
- A detailed curriculum vitae (including employment history going back at least 10 years).

A sample disclosure statement is available from the DRBF at www. drb.org. A DB nominee should also confirm and disclose to the parties involved that he or she accepts and will comply with the DRBF Code of Ethical Conduct (see Chapter 6).

Continuous Disclosure

The DRBF Code of Ethical Conduct and most DB Agreements impose an obligation of "continuous disclosure" on DB members. That is, if a

DB member's circumstances change, or if a new party is introduced into the contract or the project, the DB member will need to make a further disclosure with respect to the changed circumstances.

The parties to the contract can then make a fully informed decision as to whether the DB member's role can properly continue. Even if there is no such provision in the DB Agreement, it is good practice for DB members to make continuing disclosures as necessary, to maintain the trust and confidence of the parties.

Professional commitments of a serving DB member often change over time. For example, the DB member may be requested to serve as a DB member, arbitrator or adviser on another project in which a party (or an associate of that party) in the current engagement is involved. In all such circumstances, the DB member should seek the informed consent of the other DB members and the parties to the current contract before proceeding to accept the new appointment.

Appointment Processes

Parties selecting DB members often do not give the appointment process the time and attention it requires. Project teams frequently see the DB selection process merely as another "check the box" exercise, along with other initial contract administration tasks. However, DB selection should be regarded as one of the most important early stages of the project, since it establishes a management process for ongoing dispute avoidance and dispute resolution that will materially benefit the project.

When appointing a DB member, the nominee's qualifications and attributes relevant to the project should be carefully considered (see above and Chapter 5). Also important to consider are criteria set by the parties and any specific requirements noted in the parties' contract.

For contracts with multinational parties, nationality and pertinent language skills may also be important. When a majority of the DB members share the same nationality as one of the parties, the other "foreign" party is likely to be concerned about the DB's impartiality and independence. In such situations, it is best to appoint a DB where the majority of the DB members are of a "neutral" nationality. Both parties should feel confident that the DB is not weighted in favor of one party or the other.

DB members should be appointed at the outset of a project as a standing DB and remain in place through the project's duration. DB members thereby become familiar with the parties, the contract, and the events and circumstances that arise during the work. This knowledge makes the DB far more effective in both its dispute avoidance and resolution roles.

The initial DB meeting should be convened as soon as possible after the project contract is signed. In construction contracts, it is not uncommon for the parties' relationship to become strained early — when issues related to detailed design, constructability, site preparation and approval of management plans emerge. It is important that the DB is available at this stage to facilitate communications between the parties and to deal with issues as they arise.

Given the importance of establishing a DB at the start of a project, it is recommended that the parties' contract or the DB Agreement include a default appointment mechanism if the parties cannot agree on the DB members within a certain time. Another option is for the parties to have recourse to a nominating body (see below).

At the start of the appointment process, the parties may identify candidates for DB appointment in a variety of ways, including references from owners, contractors, consultants and other DB users; from the parties' previous DB experiences; by a search of member profiles on the DRBF website; or by issuing calls for registration of interest/request for qualifications (RFQ). A sample RFQ is available from the DRBF website at www.drb.org. It is important to note that a DB appointment is always for the individual, and it cannot be subcontracted or delegated to a corporate entity.

DB appointments occasionally depend on a competitive selection process. The design of any selection process should emphasize the required DB members' skills and experience in order to ensure properly qualified candidates. More experienced DB members will often choose not to participate where the selection criteria are based primarily on the lowest fee offer.

The list of potential DB members for a project may, in theory, be lengthy, but in practice, the list is usually restricted in some way, often by the terms of the parties' contract. In this regard, the parties may have agreed that DB members should possess specific professional qualifications or experience in the subject matter of the project. Sometimes, the contract documentation will provide a preselected list of potential DB members from which the parties can select their DB. Alternatively, institutional lists, such as those maintained by FIDIC or the ICC, can provide the contracting parties with a list of trained and accredited DB members for consideration.

Nominating a DB member from a preselected or institutional list has pros and cons. Such lists will often have minimum training and experience requirements, which enable the parties to more readily identify those who are likely to meet their DB criteria. Further, the lists may provide the names of qualified DB candidates who were previously unknown to the parties. On the other hand, these types of lists are not routinely updated and may include potential DB candidates who are unsuitable, unavailable or have conflicts of interest.

In the rush to win a project tender or to award a contract, most contractors and owners give insufficient attention to the names of their nominated DB members and their suitability for the particular project. Selection of the DB will usually be a low priority issue and a contractor is often reluctant to challenge an owner's list of DB nominees for fear that it will prejudice its tender position. Such lack of care in appointing the DB may mean the parties are stuck with DB members who are untrained, inexperienced and potentially biased.

The DRBF is able to provide lists of trained and experienced DB candidates from many of its members' countries worldwide.

Procedures for Dispute Board Member Selection

There are at least four accepted methods commonly used for selecting DB members.

Joint Selection by the Parties

In this process, the parties meet and discuss the profile of likely issues and disputes arising on the project and the qualifications of prospective DB members based on that profile. The parties then jointly select two DB members from the pool of DB nominees being considered. The parties may also select the DB Chair, which is recommended best practice. Often, however, that responsibility is left to the two selected DB members themselves.

One advantage of the joint selection method is the elimination of any perception of allegiance to a nominating party. Another advantage is that the parties can be better assured that the DB members have the necessary attributes and experience to handle issues and disputes that might arise on the project.

This method of joint selection reflects the DRBF's recommended best practice for the appointment of a DB. It has been proven to work well in many projects worldwide and across different project delivery methods, including design-build and PPP projects. For these latter delivery methods, it is important the selected DB members have specific experience and understanding of these types of projects and the skill sets that they require (for example, design or financial skills).

Nomination by Each Party

In this process, each party nominates one of the DB members and submits its nominee(s) to the other party for approval. Rather than just proposing a name (or names), a party should provide a summary of the DB nominee's expertise and explain why he or she is considered to be suitable as a DB member for the project. Likewise, the DB nominee's curriculum vitae and disclosure statement should be provided, so that the other party can assure itself that the nominee is suitable and has no actual or perceived conflicts of interest.

Once approved by the parties, the two appointed DB members then proceed to nominate the third DB member, subject to the approval of both parties. It is recommended that the parties be given the opportunity to review the third nominee's curriculum vitae and disclosure statement before approval is given (or not, as the case may be). Once approved by both parties, the third DB member often (but not automatically) serves as DB Chair.

Most agreements provide that if a DB nominee is rejected, the nominating party, within certain time frames, must nominate another candidate for consideration. Some DB Agreements further provide that if after a specified number of rounds a DB nominee is not selected, the parties must go to a neutral nominating body to make the appointment.

While the nomination of a DB member by each party is the traditional method of establishing a DB, it occasionally results in DB members who are (or are perceived to be) biased toward the nominating party. Even if a DB nominee satisfies all the selection criteria, this method of selection may in practice result in DB members being referred to as "the owner's representative" or "the contractor's representative," thereby implying a lack of independence.

Moreover, during the selection process, a party is often hesitant to reject the other party's nominee, so as to avoid disagreements during the "honeymoon" period early in the project. Another concern is when one party accepts the other party's nominee only on the condition that its own nominee be accepted.

Pre-Approved DB Lists or Panels

An alternative method of nomination is for each party to propose a list of three to six prospective DB members. Each party then selects its DB nominee from the other party's list. If a party rejects the other party's entire list, then a new list is submitted. Once selected, the two DB members then nominate the third DB member, subject to approval by both parties. The third member, not being selected by either party, will often (but not automatically) serve as DB Chair.

There are several variations to this selection method. With some projects, an alternative approach is for the contractor and owner to jointly nominate two experienced DB members. Again, with the informed consent of both the owner and contractor, those two DB members select the third DB member and then decide who will act as DB Chair.

Another related method — used by owners who routinely have several DBs operating on separate projects at any one time — is to establish an approved panel of DB members (and/or chairs). The contractor for each project is then required to select its DB nominee(s) from the owner's panel(s), subject to the usual disclosure requirements (see "Disclosure Statements" above).

Recourse to a Nominating Body

It is always preferable for the DB to be constituted by one of the consensual methods described above. However, where the parties cannot reach agreement on any or all of the members of the DB, it is important that the dispute resolution provisions within the parties' contract include a mechanism giving authority to an independent nominating body (or individual) to appoint DB members. This is particularly important for ad hoc DBs formed only when a dispute has arisen and cooperation between the parties has become degraded or nonexistent by reason of the dispute.

The nominating entity must be chosen carefully, and there are several matters to consider in this regard. First, the specified entity must be willing and able to provide a nominating service for DB members. Second, a check should be made to ensure the correct name of the nominating entity is included within the parties' contract. Third, it is important for the nominating entity to be viewed as a neutral choice.

For multi-international contracts, it is recommended that the nominating body be an international organization such as FIDIC or the ICC. For other contracts, many jurisdictions have arbitral or other professional institutions in addition to FIDIC and ICC that are willing to act as a neutral nominating body.

If a deadlock occurs in attempting to select members of a DB by consensus, and in the absence of contractual provisions for a neutral nominating entity, the parties may voluntarily seek nominations from an experienced, independent authority, such as the DRBF.

Chapter 13
Dispute Avoidance and Management

A major reason for the rapid growth of DBs worldwide is not only their success in resolving disputes quickly and efficiently but also their role in fostering dispute avoidance.

The dispute avoidance role requires a DB to undertake several fundamental tasks in overseeing a project: independently monitoring key project indicators in real time, addressing issues and potential disputes as they arise, facilitating communications between project participants and encouraging cooperative problem solving/decision making. These steps are all important in achieving the objective of a dispute-free project.

Proactive Dispute Avoidance

Feedback received by the DRBF from current projects indicates a high degree of acceptance by both owners and contractors when a DB adopts a proactive approach to its role and involvement in the project. The success of this approach generally results in a "best-for-project" outcome for all parties. DRBF members serving on these DBs regularly comment that the major part of their working time is now spent on dispute avoidance activities rather than on dispute resolution. In many of these projects, it is rare for any dispute or difference between the parties to reach the stage of a formal referral to the DB for resolution.

In addition to the direct benefits of cost and time that flow from avoidance of disputes, there are significant intangible benefits provided by regular meetings between the DB and senior project executives. DB meetings provide a forum outside the formal contractual regime for the parties to review their performance, identify current and future problems, remove roadblocks to progress and actively engage with each other in a cooperative relationship.

While these collaborative aspects of DBs are important, it is often necessary to remind project participants that the DB serves as a backstop and is not a substitute for proper contract administration and management. The parties will always be bound by the risk environment and the terms of their contract, however unfavorable that may be for one party. Notwithstanding these constraints, proactive DBs are able to facilitate communications and assist the contracting parties to deal pragmatically with the issues (commercial, technical or legal) that frequently arise in any complex set of contract conditions and specifications.

In some projects, owners seek to harness benefits of both the DB process and the Partnering process, as part of their contractual arrangements. The advantage of Partnering is that it continually focuses attention on the parties' relationships and communications, addressing day-to-day management issues that arise during the project. Partnering and the DB process, although separate in some respects, are complementary in that both processes advance dispute avoidance on the project.

While a DB can also be effective in a collaborative environment, the DB process needs to maintain a respectful distance between itself and the parties, to preserve its neutrality and maintain its objectivity. In short, Partnering and DBs can co-exist in a contract as long as the parties understand and accept the different but complementary roles inherent in the two processes.

Role of Dispute Board Members

Dispute avoidance and prevention requires DB members to take a more hands-on, inquisitorial approach, both during DB meetings and more generally during the project. Such an approach requires DB members with a high level of professional skill and experience, together with a well-developed understanding of the need for impartiality and procedural fairness in the DB's role (see Chapter 5).

For example, at the initial DB meeting with the parties, DB members should ensure they:

- Educate first-time participants on the role of the DB and how the DB proposes to implement that role on the project.
- Emphasize that the DB's role is an integral part of project governance and management.
- Stress that the DB's objective is to ensure a successful and best-for-project outcome for all parties, consistent with their contractual arrangements and obligations.
- Seek and obtain the parties' agreement to adopt DB Operating Procedures specifically directed at dispute avoidance, often amplifying the existing procedures in the DB Specification and DB Agreement.

At all subsequent DB meetings, DB members should continue to:

- Work hard to build and maintain the DB's relationship with the parties, instilling trust and confidence in the DB process and in the DB itself.
- Focus on early identification and discussion of issues arising within the project, before they become disputes.
- Encourage a collaborative approach between the parties in relation to issue resolution.
- Ensure that difficult issues are brought forward and addressed promptly, rather than being suppressed and left to fester.

There are several protocols and procedures that, if implemented by a DB, will maximize the likelihood of achieving a dispute-free project. Those aspects of the DB's work are outlined in the following sections.

Early Involvement of the Dispute Board

It is important that the DB Agreement is finalized and signed with, or shortly after, the execution of the main contract. This enables the DB to be appointed and empowered from the start of the project and before work begins.

The DRBF's experience indicates this early involvement is extremely important when the primary objective of the DB is dispute avoidance. However, early appointment alone is of little benefit unless it is accompanied by early meetings between the DB and the contracting parties. This enables the DB to establish procedures and to encourage relationship building between, and with, the parties' representatives.

Early involvement is particularly important with design-build (also known as "design-construct") contracts, where the contractor rather than the owner is responsible for the design. Experience has shown that the design phase often exposes difficult project issues and generates serious differences of opinion between the parties.

The design phase of a major design-build contract may extend from six to 12 months before any significant construction starts, so it is critical for the DB to be actively involved throughout this early period. That puts the DB in a good position to assist the parties in resolving areas of contractual ambiguity, inconsistency and requirements of performance or design standards. The DB's role at this stage often eliminates potential disputes and enables pragmatic solutions to emerge.

Amendments to Dispute Board Procedures

A key step for a newly-formed DB is to review — and in some cases, amplify or amend — the procedural rules that will apply to the project.

Even when the DB is bound by a set of standardized procedures, there are significant benefits to be gained by initially discussing DB procedures with the parties and, if appropriate, amending the procedures by agreement. This is a good way of introducing a proactive approach into an otherwise silent set of DB procedures. It also enables the DB to establish a cooperative relationship with the contracting parties and, where necessary, to define the DB's role in dispute avoidance.

Dispute Board Meeting Protocols

For regular DB meetings to be most effective, the DB Chair should implement a meeting protocol that fits within the overall governance structure for the project. In this regard, it is often established that the DB will meet with, and at the same time as, the senior executives of the contracting parties.

This protocol has the great benefit of ensuring that the senior "off-site" executives, who are commonly the only ones with the authority to make significant commercial decisions to resolve project issues, are in regular contact with both the DB and the project teams on site. The importance of establishing and maintaining these relationships for management and dispute avoidance purposes cannot be underestimated.

For regular DB meetings, the best-practice protocol being used by many DBs is to actively encourage personnel from both contracting parties to raise potential issues of concern and engage in free and frank discussions, even before any formal claim or dispute notification has been given.

The parties should also provide a regular report (often jointly) to the DB on the status of the project, the current work on site, the future work program, delays experienced, emerging commercial issues and the like. Frequently, the DB may also request one or both of the contracting parties to provide a specific report or make a presentation on a particular issue at the next DB meeting. There are many examples where this type of reporting has quickly led to negotiations and a resolution of an issue.

To encourage frankness and openness in all communications between the parties and the DB, a procedure is often implemented so that information and documents provided to the DB, as well as other documents generated within the DB process (such as minutes of DB meetings), are afforded a "confidential and privileged" or a "without prejudice" status. This latter status does not, of course, apply to documents produced by or exchanged between the parties in the normal course of project business, nor to disputes formally referred to the DB for determination.

DB members and parties should also be aware that in many civil law jurisdictions the idea of a "without prejudice" status is not recognized, except for meetings and communications exchanged strictly between the parties' counsel and without the presence of the parties. Nevertheless, this generally protective umbrella, under which DB meetings can and should be conducted, is a significant contributor to the achievement of a DB's dispute avoidance objectives.

DBs should encourage the routine scheduling of DB meetings and discourage parties who seek to delay or cancel meetings on the grounds that there are no issues or disputes to discuss. This practice, if allowed to flourish, impedes the DB from keeping up with events and circumstances on the project that may be relevant and restricts the DB's dispute avoidance role.

Advisory Opinions

Before formally referring a dispute to the DB for its decision (see Chapter 14), the parties may, by agreement, request the DB to provide an informal, nonbinding advisory opinion on an issue.

In this regard, the DB may suggest that the parties consider filing a joint request for a nonbinding opinion or assist them in formulating specific questions, the answers to which will assist in resolving the issue. This approach is commonly used by proactive DBs to provide the parties with an informal, independent, impartial and experienced view on disputed issues.

As an example, ICC Dispute Board Rules take a broad view of such informal assistance and allow the DB considerable flexibility in defining its own procedure to meet particular situations, provided both parties agree in advance to follow it.

The benefit of an advisory opinion or informal assistance is it can often be provided at short notice and focuses the attention of the parties on resolving the issue before it escalates into a dispute. The possibility of a best-for-project solution to many contentious project issues is much greater and can be facilitated by the DB if the option of an advisory opinion is readily adopted by the parties.

Chapter 14
Referral of a Dispute to the Dispute Board

Disputes should be referred to the DB when the contracting parties reach a point where a negotiated settlement cannot be reached between themselves and when the DB's dispute avoidance efforts have not borne fruit.

The contract's dispute resolution provisions should clearly spell out the steps to be followed and the conditions to be satisfied by both parties in referring a dispute to the DB. The requisite steps will vary contract to contract, but importantly, the parties should strictly follow specified time lines to obviate any possible arguments of untimely or improper notice.

Many disputes involve only questions of merit or liability, rather than quantum. If the DB makes a finding on liability and the parties accept the DB's recommendation/decision, then it is better that the parties resolve the required amount to be paid than have the DB decide it.

However, if the parties request the DB to determine quantum, the DB will be obliged to do so. In some instances, it may be appropriate for the DB to simply offer guidelines for the determination of quantum, particularly where a party has not provided enough information to enable the DB to calculate a specific quantum entitlement.

Some DB procedures provide for a two-step referral process. First, liability is determined. If merit is found, the parties then try to negotiate quantum. Secondly, if the parties cannot agree on quantum, the issue is then referred to the DB for determination. The potential bifurcation of the dispute into liability and quantum should be discussed and agreed to at the start of the DB referral process.

Notice of Referral

Referral of a dispute to the DB may be made by either the contractor or the owner. Most contracts impose specific requirements on the form and content of the Notice of Referral. If no form or content is prescribed, the Notice of Referral should concisely describe the nature and extent of the dispute being referred to the DB, as well as the determination being sought from the DB or the questions to be answered by the DB.

On receipt of the Notice of Referral, the DB should consider the terms of the referral and give the responding party an opportunity to comment. Some DB Specifications or Operating Procedures require or encourage the parties to agree on a joint statement of the issues in dispute and relief requested from the DB. This often serves to focus the issues in dispute, define the DB's jurisdiction, and avoid further disputes developing as part of the DB process itself.

Disputes Involving Third Parties

The DB Agreement is a contract between the owner, the contractor and the DB members. A subcontractor or supplier has no rights under the DB Agreement and typically will have little or no involvement in DB meetings. However, in principle and if agreed to by all parties, a DB may hear subcontractor disputes. This includes pass-through disputes from a lower-tier subcontractor or supplier against the contractor that is actionable by the contractor against the owner.

At any DB hearing on a dispute that includes subcontractor issues, each subcontractor involved in the dispute should have an authorized representative present with actual knowledge of relevant facts and available to answer any questions raised by the DB.

Disputes Over Referrals and Dispute Board Jurisdiction

The validity, interpretation and enforcement of a DB Agreement is usually governed by the laws of the state and/or country in which the contract work is performed and/or is indicated in the contract documents.

On occasion, a party may contend the DB is not authorized to hear a dispute because steps established by the contract have not been followed, the subject matter of the dispute is not appropriate for the DB process or for other reasons.

When there is disagreement between the parties about whether the DB has authority to hear a dispute, the DB should consider the contract language, the nature of the disagreement regarding jurisdiction and details of the dispute. The DB should then consider the proper course of action to resolve the jurisdictional issue by agreement with the parties.

Some DB Agreements have provisions giving the DB the power to decide on its own jurisdiction — in much the same way as arbitral tribunals are empowered to decide upon their own competence when challenged by one of the parties. Also, some project contracts provide that a DB will not have jurisdiction over some types of disputes.

Chapter 15
Prehearing Procedures and Document Preparation

Prehearing Steps

After the DB receives the Notice of Referral, either the parties or the DB may decide to hold a procedural conference to discuss how the matter referred will be addressed. In some countries, the term "conference" is preferred instead of "hearing" in the DB Operating Procedures, to lessen the possibility of the process being inadvertently exposed to local laws governing procedures for arbitrations.

The Chair, along with the other DB members and the parties, will hold a procedural conference to confirm the issues in dispute and relief requested, and establish the format and schedule for submissions prior to the hearing. This timetable should take into consideration the views and priorities of the parties concerning preparation time required for position papers and supporting exhibits.

The DB should also request that the parties make early declarations of their intentions regarding assistance from legal counsel or consultants and/or expert witnesses, to avoid an "ambush" effect later in the procedure. Some DB Operating Procedures may empower the DB to restrict the use of assistance from third parties, including lawyers.

Dates for submission of position papers, along with supporting exhibits and response papers (if agreed to by the parties), will be established in accordance with the procedure laid down in the DB Specification and/or the Operating Procedures, and/or as agreed to at the procedural conference. The estimated time for the parties to present their respective positions and for the DB to ask questions should also be discussed, so the approximate time required to conduct the hearing can be established. Most DB hearings can be scheduled so they are completed in one day.

Hearings are often conducted at the next regular DB meeting unless the matter is urgent, in which case the hearing would be scheduled sooner (as agreed to by the parties). Large or complex disputes will take more time for hearing than is likely to be available at a regular DB meeting and will need to be scheduled as a separate DB meeting.

It is good practice for the DB to request the parties to jointly prepare a Statement of Dispute, setting out an outline of their respective claims and defenses, prior to submission of their position papers. If the parties cannot agree on the Statement of Dispute, the DB should assist and/or give directions in this regard.

DBs should be aware that many contracts have short and strict time limits for rendering decisions or recommendations. Failure to respect these time limits may render the decision null and void and potentially expose DB members to liability for the costs of the process. In cases where such time limits apply, an extension is only possible with the agreement of both parties and all DB members.

Position Papers

Prior to the hearing, each party should prepare and submit to the DB and the other party factual material, legal submissions and exhibits supporting its position.

Position papers should concisely summarize the party's position, explain relevant factual information and provide a contractual justification for the position. It is important that the parties' submissions include all facts and arguments a party intends to put forth during the hearing so that the other party has the opportunity to provide a considered response paper.

Visual aids and charts, statements of evidence and (in some cases) expert reports may be included in the exhibits, but voluminous documents are discouraged. It is also beneficial for each party to address the arguments raised by the other party and explain why they believe the other party's position should not be accepted.

Position Papers in Response

Subject to the terms of the contract and/or the DB Agreement, if the parties and the DB have agreed that responsive position papers will be provided, an appropriate time should be allowed in the schedule for the provision of such submissions (sometimes called "rebuttals").

For many disputes, it is quicker and more useful for three position papers to be produced in a sequence, rather than the parties making simultaneous exchanges of both their initial position papers and/or their position papers in response. The sequence of submissions in these cases would be:

1. Claimant's position paper
2. Respondent's position paper in response, including counterclaims (if any)
3. Claimant's further reply and response to counterclaims (if any)

In determining the procedure to be followed, the DB must take care to ensure both parties' right to an equal opportunity to be heard (due process or procedural fairness) is respected.

Joint Bundle of Documents

The parties should be encouraged to jointly prepare a bundle of documents. Doing so facilitates the preparation of position papers and the DB's review and understanding of the position papers, as well as minimizing confusion and inefficiency during the hearing. In some DB Operating Procedures, this joint bundle is referred to as a Common Reference Document (CRD).

The joint bundle should include all documents either party intends to use in support of its position. Typically, the claimant compiles, in chronological order, the documents it intends to rely upon and then forwards the compilation to the respondent, who then adds, in chronological order, any other documents on which it intends to rely.

Documents inadvertently omitted from the joint bundle, or that were developed after the joint bundle was prepared, can be added later or included with the parties' respective position papers. There should be no disagreement as to what documents go into the joint bundle — whatever either party wishes to include goes in. However, irrelevant or marginally relevant documents should be excluded. Voluminous documents, such as contract conditions and specifications, should be submitted as separate volumes.

Reports from Experts, Statements from Project Personnel

Reports prepared by independent experts retained by the parties or written statements from project personnel are often attached to the parties' position papers.

If both parties have retained experts to address the matter in dispute, it is useful for the DB to request the parties' experts to prepare a joint report for the hearing. The experts' joint report should clearly identify the issues on which the experts agree and disagree. With the latter, the joint report should set out their reasons for disagreement. This procedure will enable the DB and the parties to focus on the key issues at the hearing.

Statements from project personnel are sometimes prepared by the parties to support facts asserted in their position papers. These statements are sometimes referred to as "affidavits," "statutory declarations" or "depositions," even though the DB process is not a formal legal proceeding. Regardless of what the statements are called, they should be regarded simply as a further piece of documentary information for the DB to consider.

In the hearing, DB members may wish to ask questions of the parties' respective experts or factual witnesses, but there will be no opportunity to test their evidence by cross-examination, as in a court or an arbitral tribunal (see Chapter 16).

Chapter 16
Hearing Procedures

Location, Participants

Hearings are generally conducted at a mutually acceptable location that provides the required facilities and access to additional information that might be needed at the hearing. The project site or its vicinity is generally preferred because many of the participants and necessary records are readily available.

A typical hearing requires a conference room large enough to comfortably accommodate 10 to 20 people, including the DB members, party representatives and other attendees. Electronic and other equipment should be on hand for presentations. Marker boards or flip charts may be provided to facilitate presentations. Wall space to hang drawings or charts should be available.

Participation in the hearing should be limited to senior executives from each of the contracting parties, project personnel involved in any prior negotiations and those with firsthand knowledge of the facts of the dispute. Contract administrators with roles in the management of the project — for example, a person serving as the Engineer under a FIDIC contract — should also attend.

The DB Operating Procedures will usually require the parties to advise the DB and the other party of their attendees and their roles ahead of the hearing date(s). If any proposed attendees are challenged by either party, the DB, in accordance with the agreed-upon procedure, will determine who is to participate in the hearing, as well as who may attend as an observer. The DB may also request the attendance of key personnel when such persons have knowledge that will assist the DB in its deliberations.

Although the attendance of lawyers at DB hearings is often unnecessary, some DB Operating Procedures allow them to participate in the hearing or alternatively provide for their attendance, possibly as only observers. For more complex disputes, particularly those involving questions of contractual liability and interpretation, the attendance of the parties' legal representatives will usually be of assistance to the DB. Some DB Rules/Operating Procedures empower the DB to exclude nonparty attendees; however, such powers of exclusion should be used sparingly and with discretion.

The Hearing

Prior to the hearing date(s), the DB Chair should prepare and transmit to the parties an agenda for the hearing, establishing the sequence of steps in the process with an explanation of how the hearing will be conducted.

The DB Chair often holds a prehearing conference call or meeting with party representatives to review logistics for the hearing and address any issues of concern. The purpose of this prehearing meeting should be to set up the hearing to be procedurally fair and efficient.

DB hearings must be conducted in a manner that encourages frankness, openness and the thorough disclosure of all pertinent information bearing on the dispute. DB members should ask questions whenever necessary to obtain all the facts and ensure that they fully understand the parties' respective positions, the facts of the case and the parties' contentions regarding entitlement, as put forward in their written submissions.

The DB should also allow party questioning to the extent it assists in getting all facts "on the table." This is usually handled by a request to the Chair, who will decide whether and how the question is addressed.

Hearing presentations may include a summary of position papers, discussion and explanation of supporting information and presentation of visual aids and demonstrative evidence. These presentation materials should be submitted in advance of the hearing so as to avoid "surprise" at the hearing or disputes over what is presented.

There must be adequate time to ensure each party has the opportunity to be fully heard and the DB is satisfied it understands each party's position, supporting arguments and facts surrounding the dispute.

Typically, the hearing follows an agreed-upon sequence: The claimant makes its presentation first, followed by the respondent's presentation. The next stage consists of questions from DB members followed by rebuttals from each party. The parties may also be allowed to make a final oral summary at the end of the hearing. The DB must be satisfied that all relevant information has been presented for its consideration.

Importantly, the DB hearing is not a judicial process — oaths are not administered, legal rules of evidence are not observed, and cross-examination of witnesses or direct, party-to-party questioning is not permitted except at the discretion of the DB. There may be occasions where it is appropriate for the DB to allow a party to raise a question to be addressed by the other party, upon request for permission to do so. In addition, a joint discussion, led by the DB, is commonly permitted as a useful way to ascertain the facts or expert opinions in an efficient manner.

Sometimes, a party will produce information at the hearing for the first time, either as a surprise tactic or because the information had been previously neglected. Although this behavior should be discouraged, if additional information has been developed or come to light after submission of the position papers, the DB should permit this information to be introduced. The other party should be given ample time to consider and respond to it. This may cause the hearing to be adjourned, with consequent delay and additional costs. In all such situations, the governing rule is that both parties should be treated fairly and equally.

If it becomes apparent during the hearing that either party has not addressed an important fact in the dispute or a key provision of the contract documents, the DB should ask both parties for their positions on that issue. If this situation is discovered after the hearing, both parties should be asked to address the issue in writing.

Similarly, if at the conclusion of the hearing the DB believes additional documentation or other information is required to understand the issues, it may request that such information be submitted by the parties.

In this case, the hearing is left open pending receipt of the additional materials. It is usually unnecessary to reconvene the hearing; however, this is a possibility depending on several factors: the nature of the additional materials received, the available time remaining under applicable time limits for the DB decision or recommendation and the DB's perception of the need for such additional information.

Refusal by a Party to Attend

If one party refuses to attend a hearing, the DB must decide whether to proceed with the hearing in the absence of that party, to postpone the hearing or to cancel it altogether.

Some DB Rules/Operating Procedures provide that the hearing may continue even if one of the parties fails to appear. One of the factors that must be considered is whether the refusing party has a valid reason for nonappearance, such as needing additional time to prepare its case. The DB also must consider whether the party is unwilling to participate for reasons directed at obstructing the DB process.

In any event, the DB has a contractual obligation by virtue of the DB Agreement to provide a forum for hearing disputes. Sometimes the referring party is precluded by the contract from pursuing dispute resolution measures unless the DB dispute resolution process has been strictly followed. If this is the case, the DB must proceed with the hearing despite non-attendance by one of the parties. The DB will render its findings based on the facts made available to it by the attending party as well as any prehearing documentation submitted by the non-attending party.

When proceeding with a hearing without one of the parties present, the DB should take steps to ensure that the nonparticipating party's right to procedural fairness is safeguarded.

The DB should make persistent efforts to be sure the party has been informed of the time and place of the hearing. The DB should attempt to contact the nonattending party at the outset of the hearing to ascertain its reason for not attending. The DB should also limit the submission of any new evidence or arguments by the attending party to only essential matters and afford the nonattending party an opportunity to respond after the hearing.

It is important that the DB asks probing questions of key factual assertions advanced by the attending party, which may seem lacking in evidentiary support. The DB should not, however, attempt to advocate in the place of the nonattending party. In some cases, it is recommended to arrange for a transcript to be made of the hearing and to give the transcript to the nonattending party after the hearing.

Chapter 17
Recommendations and Decisions

The DB is required to publish its findings in the form of a DB Report, which may be a nonbinding recommendation, a binding decision or an interim binding decision. The latter is a decision binding on the parties unless contested by one party within a certain specified time.

Dispute Board Deliberations after the Hearing

Dispute resolution provisions in contract documents or the DB Operating Procedures will usually include a time period within which the DB is expected to issue its findings. If not, a time period should be agreed to by the parties. If the time is insufficient to prepare the DB Report, based on the DB members' availability or the complexity of the dispute, the DB should make a written request to the parties to extend the date. In most cases, the DB may not extend any contractually stipulated time limits without both parties' consent. It is important that DBs adhere to these timelines, given a goal of the DB process is to promote efficient and cost-effective dispute resolution.

After the hearing has been concluded, the DB will meet privately to discuss the information and submissions presented by the parties. If all three DB members have generally similar conclusions, the main effort will be directed toward composing the DB Report. If not, one or more sessions between DB members may be needed to reconcile differences. Deliberations should be concluded as soon as practicable. Care should be exercised to ensure privacy and confidentiality.

Objectives of deliberations prior to issuing the DB Report include:

- Understanding and analyzing the merits of the parties' positions.
- Finding and agreeing on relevant facts.
- Reaching agreement on applicability and interpretation of relevant contract requirements.

- Agreeing on the DB's findings with respect to the issues and questions posed by the parties.
- Drafting the DB Report so the findings and supporting analysis/reasoning are straightforward, easy to understand and responsive to submissions made by the parties.

Immediately after the hearing, if time allows and DB members are available, it is useful for initial deliberations to be held and an outline of the DB Report prepared. Later, drafts of the DB Report can be exchanged among DB members until full agreement is reached. The DB Chair usually takes the lead in organizing the DB Report and having it completed on schedule. For complex disputes with many issues to address, the drafting work will often be divided among DB members.

If, during deliberations, the need arises for additional information, such as copies of documents not in the DB's possession, a request may be made to either party. The additional information must be provided to the other party as well as to the DB. The DB should then consider any additional information provided, with both parties being given the opportunity to respond.

The Dispute Board Report

DB findings, analysis and recommendations or decisions that constitute the DB Report must be based on the information and submissions presented by the parties, in accordance with relevant provisions of the contract, and with due regard for applicable laws and regulations.

It is important that DB members thoroughly consider all applicable provisions of the contract when preparing the DB Report. Depending on the facts and circumstances of the dispute, the DB may also need to consider relevant industry codes, practices and standards, expert opinions and legal submissions.

As with the DB's obligation to keep its findings within the boundaries of the contract documents, the DB must confine its recommendations and decisions to the issues in dispute as it has no jurisdiction to determine other issues.

The parties may pose questions to the DB in their position papers. Well-considered answers to such questions may be critical to the resolution of the dispute. The DB should respond to these questions to the extent reasonable and necessary.

It is often helpful to include in the DB Report a chronology of events and a summary of both parties' positions, including references to relevant sections of the contract cited by each party in support of their respective positions.

It is fundamental that DBs must not recommend a compromise settlement or make decisions according to what they believe would be acceptable or fair to both parties. Individual notions of "fairness" or "equity" have no place in the DB process. The DB's findings must be in accordance with facts and circumstances presented, contract documents, and applicable law and regulations.

In drafting the DB Report, the DB should explain the reasoning behind its findings and conclusions on each issue. This is best accomplished by demonstrating that all significant points raised in the parties' position papers and during the hearing have been considered. Every important point from each party's position should be summarized and addressed.

The DB's reasoning should be fully explained in a clear and logical sequence so both parties can understand and accept the outcome. The DB should not disparage either party's position or presentation. That approach may not only be unhelpful in resolving the dispute but may give rise to concerns about lack of impartiality.

The DB Report should be neither extremely brief, with little explanation, nor long and verbose, with pages of material having little relevance to issues in dispute. The DB Report should be concise and to the point, yet detailed enough for representatives of either party to adequately understand the reasoning supporting the recommendations or decisions of the DB. The DB Report must be professional, objective and impersonal.

Minority Decisions

The aim of a DB should always be to produce a unanimous DB Report. By thoroughly reviewing and exploring one another's perspectives and by reasonable compromise, DB members can almost always reach unanimity and prepare a DB Report acceptable to all three DB members.

When publishing a DB Report, dissenting opinions should be discouraged and should be provided only when the dissenting DB member strongly disagrees with the majority opinion. A dissenting opinion is unlikely to assist the parties in resolving their dispute.

If, however, despite the DB's best efforts, it is unable to reach a unanimous conclusion, the dissenting member should prepare a minority conclusion with supporting rationale. This minority opinion is then included in the DB Report along with the majority opinion. The identity of the dissenting DB member should not be revealed. Instead, all three DB members should sign the DB Report, with the minority conclusion set forth as a separate section so identified.

Clarifications and Further Consideration

If the DB Report contains a clerical mistake, an accidental error or omission; a material miscalculation of figures; a material mistake in the description of any person, matter or thing; or a defect in form, the DB must correct the decision if requested by one of the parties. The other party should then be given an opportunity to respond to the request.

Occasionally a party may request correction of what it considers to be a clerical error but, in fact, is nothing more than an attempt to reopen the dispute. In such circumstances, the DB should decline to be drawn into any reconsideration of the DB's findings.

Chapter 18

Implementation of the Dispute Board's Findings

A DB may be requested to provide an advisory opinion, a nonbinding recommendation or a binding decision. This chapter examines each of these options, how the parties may best utilize them and the enforcement of the DB's findings.

Advisory Opinions

The concept of a DB providing the parties with an advisory opinion is included in many DB specifications as a means of invoking DB participation in dispute avoidance. Even when not expressly provided for in the DB Specification, the parties will often request a DB to provide an advisory opinion on an issue or potential dispute. This option for addressing a contested question is quicker and less costly than proceeding through the steps of a DB hearing to obtain a DB Recommendation or DB Decision.

Advisory opinions are well-suited to situations where there appears to be a stumbling block impeding the parties' negotiation of a contested issue, such as interpretation of a particular contract term or specification provision.

Such advisory opinions, expressing the DB's preliminary views, often facilitate resolution of the issue without further assistance from the DB. However, advisory opinions are of little use in resolving some claims. If the issue is not resolved by negotiation and is referred to a DB hearing, it is important to understand that the parties will not be bound by earlier presentations or positions, and that the DB is not bound by preliminary views it may have expressed.

The parties will often ask for an advisory opinion to be put in writing, with supporting reasons, so that the opinion can be used by one or both parties to facilitate a resolution by senior executives with higher authority. Or, the opinion can be added to project records as justification for the resolution reached. In some limited circumstances, it may be appropriate for the DB to simply provide an oral advisory opinion, but the DB should bear in mind that such oral advice can easily be misconstrued or ignored.

Nonbinding Recommendations

In the U.S. and some other countries, nonbinding recommendations are most commonly used. Often, DBs are asked initially to address only merit or liability issues. Later, if the dispute is still unresolved, the parties may ask the DB to provide suggested guidelines for resolving quantum issues rather than hearing the entire dispute. DBs may wish to suggest this option if it believes it can save costs and time for the parties.

With this option, parties are typically required to accept or reject the recommendation within a defined time period. Some contracts require the rejecting party to state its reasons, with the objective of supporting later negotiations. In addition, a failure to reject a recommendation within a specified period results in deemed acceptance. DRBF research indicates that even in those cases of rejection, the parties often used the DB's Recommendation in the negotiation and resolution of the dispute without further proceedings.

In U.S. practice, an important consideration within DB specifications is whether the DB Recommendation, while not binding, should be admissible in evidence and considered by a subsequent tribunal, in the event the parties proceed to binding dispute resolution through arbitration or court litigation.

Supporters of admissibility believe any subsequent tribunal is likely to give significant weight to the findings of a DB composed of persons selected by the parties and having ongoing contact with the project. DB members would have detailed knowledge of the facts, relevant experience and greater expertise in the dispute's subject matter than members of the tribunal. The further argument for admissibility is that DB recommendations will have more "teeth," that is, will be taken more seriously by the parties (possibly leading to a settlement), when the DB Recommendation is highly likely to be persuasive in a subsequent binding proceeding.

The argument against admissibility is that it is likely to change the character of the DB dispute resolution process, resulting in greater formality, hardening of positions and a reduced cooperative atmosphere, all of which will negatively affect the relationship of the parties going forward.

Supporters of nonadmissibility argue that the fundamental purpose of the DB process is to assist the parties in avoiding and resolving disputes at the project level. What might happen at a later stage, outside the project, should not influence the DB's recommendation/decision and vice versa. This view is based on the reality that the decision of a subsequent tribunal may well be made with the benefit of discovery of both parties' documents and on the basis of different and more extensive evidence than available to the DB during its process.

In this ongoing debate, the DRBF supports and recommends admissibility over nonadmissibility as the best-practice approach. Most DB users (both contractors and owners) also support admissibility.

Interim Binding Decisions

Many contracts and DB specifications provide that a DB Decision will be binding and enforceable unless or until modified or overturned by a higher authority, such as an arbitration award or a court judgment.

This approach is more common in international practice than in the U.S. and is used in particular with FIDIC contracts (see Chapter 9). This means a DB Decision with an award in favor of one party is required to be implemented immediately by the other party. If an arbitral tribunal or court later overturns the award, the awarded amount must be repaid. Enforcement and implementation of interim binding decisions sometimes proves problematic in practice and is discussed further below.

Final and Binding Decisions

Relatively few DB specifications provide that a DB decision will be final and binding and not subject to appeal to a higher authority. More commonly, DB specifications provide that a DB decision will be final and binding only if it is not objected to or appealed to an arbitral tribunal or court within a (relatively short) specified period of time.

In some jurisdictions, a final and binding DB decision will be accorded the same force and effect as an arbitration award. More often, however, a final and binding DB decision needs to be converted to an arbitration award if it is to be the subject of judicial enforcement proceedings.

Many countries, including the U.S., have entered into multilateral treaties (e.g., The New York Convention) providing for the enforcement of foreign arbitration awards. However, the DRBF is not aware of any jurisdictions having enacted laws specifically governing DBs. Thus far, DB procedures and decisions have been solely a matter for the private contract law of the governing legal jurisdiction.

Enforcement in Different Legal Jurisdictions

It is difficult to categorize the approaches to enforcement of DB decisions in different legal jurisdictions for two reasons. First, there are few reported instances of attempts to enforce decisions, and second, the laws of legal jurisdictions vary in how they address enforcement.

Any enforcement attempt will be specific to the case and jurisdiction and must be guided by experienced legal counsel in that jurisdiction. Anecdotally, however, it seems that final and binding decisions are often enforced relatively quickly in many jurisdictions, and there is a growing trend of a "pay now, arbitrate later" approach to enforcement of interim binding decisions.

Factors in most jurisdictions that influence appeals against enforcement of DB decisions are whether:

- Procedural rights of the dissatisfied party were adequately protected during the DB process.
- The decision on its face is rational and not contrary to the contract, the facts or applicable law.
- The decision is inconsistent with the public policy of the country in question.

There are three situations where a **DB Decision** is not likely to be enforced:

- The decision is principally based on subjective factors, such as fairness and equity, rather than on facts and applicable law.
- There is insufficient reasoning or explanation of how the decision was reached, or there appears to be no more than an arbitrary compromise between the respective parties.
- The hearing process was conducted in a procedurally unfair way.

Chapter 19

Review, Termination or Renewal of the Dispute Board

Most DBs are established when a project begins and remain in place until the project is completed. As a result, the life of a DB often spans several years, during which time events may occur that result in the resignation of a DB member or a request from a party to terminate a DB member or the entire DB. Historical reasons for such terminations or resignations include:

- One or both parties' dissatisfaction with the DB's performance, its findings or another aspect of its work.
- A DB member's conflict of interest, apparent bias or other nonethical behavior.
- The continuing unavailability of a DB member, often because of other work commitments, health problems or even death.
- A DB member no longer wishing to continue serving on the DB for personal or professional reasons.

Factors to Consider with Termination or Resignation

A decision on termination or resignation is often difficult for the DB, and the outcome can be controversial and harmful to the DB process. Several factors, including those discussed below, should be considered in deciding whether to terminate, resign from and/or renew a DB.

If a DB member is terminated or resigns, the loss can be significant, particularly if it occurs at a key stage of the project. The project loses valuable knowledge and experience that the DB member has gained about the project, the contract, events that have occurred and the people involved.

Furthermore, if one of the parties appointed the DB member, the party may feel it will be somehow prejudiced by the loss. As a result, both the parties and the DB should avoid premature loss of a DB member whenever possible.

It is fundamental to the success of a DB that each DB member establishes a relationship of trust with the parties. If a party loses confidence in a member, the DB's ability to perform its functions on the project can be seriously eroded. The DB's effectiveness in avoiding and resolving disputes between the parties is diminished if there is a lack of trust. Confidence and trust in the DB lie at the heart of a successful DB process. In most cases, the need for the DB to maintain a good relationship with the parties will outweigh all other considerations when decisions have to be made regarding termination and resignation.

On the other hand, the DB should be aware of the possibility that one of the parties may not be acting in good faith in seeking termination of the DB or the resignation of a DB member. Rather, that party may be attempting to game the system by changing the makeup of the DB to obtain more favorable outcomes, particularly where DB decisions adversely affect that party and may be admissible in subsequent court proceedings (see Chapter 18). If such party behavior emerges, the DB Chair or another DB member may need to counsel senior executives of the contracting parties (those external to the project) to regain the parties' continuing cooperation in the DB process.

Termination or Resignation?

If a party is dissatisfied with a DB member or the entire DB, it should first consult the DB Agreement to determine what actions are possible. The DB Agreement will usually include provisions that govern termination, resignation and reappointment of DB members.

Some DB Agreements allow a party to unilaterally terminate the appointment of a DB member. However, unilateral termination gives rise to several difficulties and is not considered to be a best practice by DRBF.

Most DB Agreements usually provide that individual DB members (or the DB as a whole) may be terminated only by agreement of both contracting parties. As a result, if one party wants to terminate a DB member, it must first attempt to reach agreement on the termination of that member with the other party, and then jointly request that the member resign.

The parties should refer the issue to the DB Chair (or the DB as an entity), particularly if the basis of the challenge results from alleged impropriety or ethical violations by the DB member. In cases where both parties agree that the DB member should resign, the consent of the DB or its Chair is not necessary.

The DB should always be sensitive to any appearance of bias or impropriety in its dealings with the parties and to any obvious disillusionment by a party with the DB or a DB member. If the DB senses a problem or the dissatisfaction of a party, it should be proactive and raise the issue with the parties.

If a party is concerned about partiality or conduct of the DB or a DB member, all DB members should treat the matter seriously. The DB should have candid conversations with the parties and seek to resolve the matter. Unilateral conversations are allowed in these circumstances, and the outcome of these conversations should be shared with all parties.

Replacement of Dispute Board Members

Difficulties involved with removing and replacing DB members highlight the importance of initially selecting properly qualified, independent, impartial and ethical DB members (see Chapter 12). It is far better for the parties to properly consider requirements of the project first and then research the qualifications, experience and availability of proposed DB members. Such an approach is also much better than automatically accepting a nominated DB member and later having to deal with the problems of termination and finding a suitable replacement.

If a DB member is terminated or resigns for any reason, the DB Agreement will usually contain provisions enabling that DB member to be replaced. These provisions will include either renomination by the contractor or owner if it is one of their nominees who has resigned or been removed, or renomination by the remaining two DB members.

Consent of all parties is required before a replacement DB member can be accepted and take his or her place on the DB. The new DB member will be required to enter into the DB Agreement. He or she should then review both the minutes of DB meetings to date and any decisions or recommendations issued by the DB, and generally be brought up to speed on the project by the other DB members.

In some circumstances, particularly late in the project, when a resignation or removal occurs, the owner, contractor and remaining DB members may see no need to search for and agree upon a replacement. While this is a practical matter for the parties, in most circumstances it is desirable to appoint a new DB member to fill the open position, so that the DB remains fully and properly constituted until the end of its term.

Termination or Resignation of the Dispute Board

On occasion, one or both parties may become dissatisfied or lose interest in the DB process — to the extent that they cancel meetings, do not engage with the DB for the purposes of avoiding disputes, reject DB opinions or recommendations with respect to disputes and/or become generally uncooperative.

Even if there is no rational basis for such dissatisfaction, the lack of trust and confidence in the DB process can reduce the value of the DB to the point where it may be in the best interest of the project for the entire DB to resign. Whether a replacement DB is to be appointed is an important consideration at this point. Nevertheless, in all such cases, maintaining the integrity and efficacy of the DB process should take precedence over the resigning DB members' subjective views.

If an entire DB is replaced, either because of voluntary resignation or termination by the parties, the DB should not perform any further work other than completing unfinished tasks. Such tasks include recommendations and decisions on previously referred disputes and for which submissions and hearings have been completed.

Previous recommendations and decisions that have been accepted by both parties should not be revisited by a new DB. However, a request by the parties for a new DB to re-examine previous disputes that remain unresolved may, in some circumstances, assist in resolving these matters within the project rather than proceeding to litigation or arbitration.

Renewal of the Dispute Board after Completion

Most DB Agreements provide for the DB to cease operating at the completion of the project. However, the definition of completion and the DB's role after completion may depend on the terms of the project contract. For example, FIDIC DBs are obliged to stay in place until the Defects Notification Period has expired, since disputes and issues such as latent defects may still arise for resolution. In these circumstances, maintaining the standing of the DB (even if it is suspended) will give the parties the potential benefit of the DB's knowledge and experience and allow the DB to assist the parties in resolving any outstanding disputes.

In addition, if the project is ongoing (such as a maintenance contract renewed annually), or if the project is constructed in phases (sometimes over several years), provision should be made for the renewal of the DB each year or at the start of each phase. In these instances, the DB Agreement should provide that the DB or a DB member's term is limited to a specified time period. This provision also makes sense for projects with a long duration or when a project is continuing for an unlimited period.

Glossary

Ad hoc Dispute Board: A DB that is constituted only for purposes of a dispute being referred to it for resolution. This type of DB usually has a restricted role and a limited period of operation.

Advisory Opinion: A reasoned opinion, which is often in writing, issued by the DB in response to a request from the parties. Advisory opinions are non-binding on the parties and the DB. An advisory opinion provides the parties with the DB's preliminary views on the resolution of an issue prior to it being referred to the DB as a dispute.

Board Member: *See* ***DB member****.*

CDB: The abbreviation for a Combined Dispute Board, as used under the ICC Rules.

Chair: The DB member who manages and coordinates the DB's activities, chairs DB meetings and acts as the primary point of contact between the parties and the DB.

Contractor: The party (or more than one party as a joint venture) that has entered into a contract with the project owner to perform a specified scope of work or services as defined in the project agreement.

DAAB: The abbreviation for a Dispute Avoidance and Adjudication Board, as used in FIDIC forms of contract.

DAB: The abbreviation for a Dispute Adjudication Board or a Dispute Avoidance Board.

DB: The common abbreviation used in this manual for Dispute Boards of all types.

DB Agreement: A contractual agreement between the parties (owner and contractor) and the DB members, different from the project agreement. This agreement establishes the role, authority and obligations of the DB members and the parties. This agreement is sometimes referred to as a Three-Party Agreement or as a Tri-Partite Agreement (TPA).

DB Decision: The DB's findings following the referral of a dispute to the DB.

A DB Decision is binding (or interim binding) on the parties, in contrast to a DB Recommendation or an advisory opinion. A DB Decision should be in writing and set out the DB's analysis and reasoning in support of its findings on the dispute.

DB Determination: *See* **DB Decision**.

DB meeting: The regular meeting between the DB and the parties to review the status and progress of work, to address issues that have arisen between the parties. A site visit is often held in conjunction with the DB meeting.

DB member: A formally appointed member of the DB, after he/she has been nominated and agreed to by the parties and has signed the DB Agreement.

DB nominee: A prospective member of the DB who has been nominated but is yet to be formally appointed and sign the DB Agreement.

DB Operating Procedures: Procedures that the DB members and the parties have agreed to follow for the duration of the project. DB Operating Procedures often include meeting arrangements, communication protocols, dispute avoidance techniques, detailed requirements for the conduct of a DB hearing and the DB's decision-making functions. The DB Operating Procedures are usually addressed within the DB Specification or the DB Agreement.

DB Recommendation: *See* **DB Decision**. A DB Recommendation is essentially the same as a DB Decision, except that it is non-binding on the parties. In some cases, a DB Recommendation may become a binding DB Decision if not objected to within a specified period of time.

DB Report: A DB Report is the document issued by the DB that sets out the DB's advisory opinion, DB Decision or DB Recommendation, as the case may be.

DB Specification: The DB Specification usually documents the overall DB process, including establishment of the DB, the selection and appointment of DB members and the responsibilities of DB members in both their dispute avoidance and dispute resolution roles.

Design-build (D&B): A form of contract where the owner contracts with a single entity to perform both the design and construction work for a project. In some countries, this form of contract is referred to as "Design and Construct" or "DB" (not to be confused with the abbreviation for "Dispute Board").

Disclosure statement: Statement submitted by a DB nominee disclosing any actual or potential conflicts of interest or other relevant information. The disclosure allows the parties to determine whether the DB nominee meets the necessary standards of independence and impartiality.

Dispute: An issue between the parties that has not been avoided or amicably resolved and is formally referred to the DB for a DB Decision or DB Recommendation. *Also see **Joint Statement of Dispute** and **Notice of Referral**.* Note that in the management of many contracts, the general word "dispute" is frequently used by contracting parties to describe any disagreement or difference between them.

Dispute Resolution Clause: A provision within the project agreement that establishes an overall dispute resolution process, as well as the role and functions of the DB within the project's governance structure.

DRA: The abbreviation for a Dispute Resolution Advisor.

DRB: The abbreviation for a Dispute Review Board or a Dispute Resolution Board.

Employer: *See **Owner**.* This term is used in FIDIC forms of contract.

Engineer: This term is used in FIDIC forms of contract. The Engineer is generally the Employer's agent, except when required to make an independent determination of a disputed issue.

EPC: The abbreviation for an Engineering, Procurement and Construction form of contract.

Ex parte communication: A communication (written or oral) between a DB Member and one of the parties, without the knowledge or presence of the other party.

Facilitation: An informal process in which the DB assists the parties to amicably resolve an issue between them by facilitating discussion, evaluation of positions and/or the provision of an advisory opinion.

FIDIC: The acronym for the Fédération Internationale des Ingénieurs-Conseils, which translates in English to the International Federation of Consulting Engineers.

GMP: The abbreviation for a Guaranteed Maximum Price.

ICC: The acronym for the International Chamber of Commerce. The ICC publishes Dispute Board Rules and standard DB clauses for contracts.

IFI: The acronym for an International Financing Institution, which refers to organizations such as development banks and funding agencies. IFIs often have a mandatory requirement for the inclusion of a DB in projects they fund.

Initial DB meeting: The initial meeting between the DB and the parties to provide information and details about the project, to explain the role of the DB and to discuss and agree upon the DB Operating Procedures (if not already specified) and the administrative arrangements for the DB.

Issue: An unresolved disagreement or difference of opinion between the parties, often arising as a claim for time, money, defective work, or other relief by a party. An issue is a necessary precursor to a matter becoming a dispute.

MDB: The abbreviation for a Multilateral Development Bank, such as the World Bank. *Also see **IFI**.*

Notice of Referral: A document that defines the dispute being referred to the DB and triggers the resolution procedure. The notice may be submitted by either the owner or the contractor. The formal requirements of the notice will usually be stipulated within the Dispute Resolution Clause in the project agreement.

Owner: The entity that has entered into a contract with the contractor. In many places outside North America, the owner is referred to as the employer or the principal.

Owner's Representative (or **Superintendent**): *See **Engineer**.* In many contracts, the owner's representative is solely an agent and generally does not have any independent decision-making powers.

Parties: The parties to the project agreement – typically, the owner and the contractor.

Partnering: A project management concept in which the owner, designer and contractor meet together regularly during the duration of the project to improve communications, build teamwork and prevent adversarial relationships from developing.

Party: One of the parties to the project agreement – typically, either the owner or the contractor.

Position Papers: Documents prepared by each party for submission to the DB. Position papers are intended to concisely summarize each party's position, explain relevant factual information, and provide contractual justification for a party's position.

Procedural fairness: Requirement that each of the parties be given a fair and reasonable opportunity to be heard, to adequately present their respective cases and to adequately respond to any issue or dispute that may arise between them.

Public-Private Partnership (PPP or P3): A form of project delivery for public infrastructure projects. These types of projects are funded wholly or in part by private entities. These forms of contract are between a government entity and a private partner, which can be a privately-owned company, a public corporation, or a consortium of business entities.

Quantum: The amount of money claimed by one party from the other party, pursuant to relevant provisions of the project agreement.

Request for qualifications (RFQ): A prequalification step for DB nominees, in which persons interested in appointment to the DB for a project are asked to submit a statement of their interest and ability to perform the DB duties.

Site visit: The segment of a regular DB meeting during which the DB members can inspect and observe the progress of the work on the project site, accompanied by representatives of the owner and contractor.

Special Purpose Vehicle (SPV): A term used within PPP projects to describe the legal entity set up solely for the purposes of delivering the project. The SPV enters into separate contracts with both the project procuring authority and the design-build contractor.

Statement of Dispute: A concise statement of the matter in dispute which has been referred to the DB for its Decision or Recommendation, as jointly agreed by the parties.

Third-Party Stakeholders: A third party stakeholder is a party with a financial or other interest in a project but is not a party to the contract between the owner and contractor.

Three-Party Agreement or Tri-Partite Agreement (TPA): *See* *DB Agreement.*

Index